The Teacher's Charge:

Readjusting the Educational Point of View

BY

BENJAMIN SKINNER, M.A., F.E.I.S.,
President of the Educational Institute of Scotland, 1923-1924

———————

THE EDUCATIONAL INSTITUTE OF SCOTLAND
47 MORAY PLACE, EDINBURGH

———

Price Two Shillings and Sixpence

Printed and Published for the Educational Institute of Scotland
by Lindsay & Co., 17 Blackfriars Street, Edinburgh

FOREWORD.

"Scottish Educational Journal" Office,
47 Moray Place, Edinburgh.

PRESS, platform and pulpit continually tell us that education is a matter of prime importance to every citizen. That this commonplace of rhetoric and conversation is a general rule of conduct is shown by the great willingness with which most people discourse on education, its purpose, its methods and, most abundantly, its shortcomings. No public man, be he cleric or layman, novelist or successful manufacturer, statesman or newspaper proprietor, but has his views on the subject and a surprising facility in imparting these to his fellow-Britons. This, I believe, works ultimately, if not wholly, for the greater good of the commonweal. It reveals a degree of interest that augurs well for continued progress in the most difficult of all arts—the art of training the men and women of the future.

Yet, while the observer, the amateur, has a right to examine, comment, criticise and suggest, it may fairly be urged that the people whose opinions are most likely to be worth listening to are those whose lives are spent in the service of that art. It is true that their natures are liable to be subdued to their medium, that they are prone to show the characteristics of their semi-cloistered profession, that they inevitably betray the *differentia* of a separate caste. Nevertheless it is only by them that the continual adaptation of educational methods to social ends, upon which in the last resort national progress depends, can be carried out.

It is not merely professional *esprit-de-corps*, therefore, that makes me regard this book by my friend, Mr Skinner, as significant. Here is a teacher of ripe experience, of proved

FOREWORD.

capacity, taking his fellow-citizens into his confidence and letting them know what he thinks of Scottish education as it actually is, and his hopes and plans for its advancement. Mr Skinner has earned the right to be heard by his long, faithful and highly successful career as a teacher. He is one to whom his professional brethren turn frequently, and never in vain, for wise counsel and effective leading. I am sure that the general public will learn much from the chapters in which he has recorded the lessons he has learned during a lifetime of devoted study of the art of education.

THOMAS HENDERSON.

CONTENTS.

The Teacher's Charge.

T HE success of any system of Education depends on several factors, one of the most important of which is the quality of the pupils. Progress in securing their physical, social and intellectual improvement must necessarily be slow, but there can be little doubt that the efforts now being made towards betterment will be more than justified in the long-run. The other outstanding factor is the teacher. In theory nearly every one, even the least to feel that they are trusted, experience has abundantly proved that they may safely be relied on to do their part in the educational economy. Writing as one who has had the privilege for many years of knowing Scottish teachers of every class and grade, I am sure that the teaching profession is ready to co-operate in securing the continual re-adapting of means to ends that changing circumstances demand. The responsibility that properly belongs to the profession will, I am convinced, increase in proportion as liberal views of education, principles and methods become more prevalent. I propose, therefore, to deal at the outset with the teacher's charge, and to conclude with the complimentary topic, the teacher's support.

There are few words in the English language richer in meanings than the word charge. Without entering into all the shades and differences, let me say at once that for my present purpose I take charge to mean load or responsibility, precisely what is meant in the clerical profession when a man is admitted into the ministry by some definite ceremony of ordination and receives a charge. Some may think it a pity that teachers are not thus specifically set apart, but there may be—in my opinion there are—real compensations. A commission hemmed in by over-strict conditions, and couched in language that tends to become archaic or even meaningless, is apt to hamper and may even gall. Better perhaps, in the teaching profession at least, to have no ritual of setting apart; to be open to receive inspiration and guidance from the increasing light that individual and collective experience brings to the open-minded.

The Teacher's Charge may for our present purpose be divided into four portions, distinct indeed but clearly related. These four constituent elements are: the interests of the pupil; the promotion of sound learning; the culture and welfare of the teaching profession, together with the maintenance of its dignity; the interest of the community and the service of the State.

Not without reason do we place the interests of the pupil first. In every reasonable system of education, and at every stage, the pupils' interests are first and paramount. The pupil is the centre. Any system, however superficially attractive, however specious, that dethrones the pupil and exalts administration, curriculum, preparation for the making of a living, the advantage of the State narrowly interpreted, stands self-condemned, and must be strenuously opposed.

What do we mean by the pupil?

For purposes of definition and classification we speak of the average or normal pupil, and above and below him we arrange other classes such as super-normal and sub-normal, brilliant and dull. Such enumerations and classifications may be advisable or even necessary in the eyes of those who pride themselves on being logical and systematic. There is, however, in this connection, a danger that we may err if we imagine that our classifications are more than tentative and experimental. We cannot assess spiritual values by material standards. Inside and outside school there are those who confidently affirm that only certain pupils are educable. The teacher who has a cast-iron system; the short-sighted parent who says that the child is his own and proceeds to deprive his son of his birthright in the matter of education; the stingy ratepayer who objects to expenditure on education on the ground that posterity has never done anything for him —these find themselves in agreement on this point if on no other. The teacher of a by-gone age had one great merit in the eyes of those who eulogise the dead only after they have passed to where they hear no words of praise or blame.

He is said to have had a theory of education. The subjects
of the curriculum were definitely and unalterably fixed; the
order and the methods of study were invariable. Pupils who
could not adapt themselves or be by some forcible means
adapted to those methods were not worth consideration. It
is not my intention at present to enter into a controversy as
to the comparative merits and demerits of existing teachers
and their predecessors in the science and art of teaching, but
it may be safely affirmed that an age that has exalted the
claims of the child as ours has done and is doing, has titles
to credit, which alleged though unsubstantiated charges
of degeneracy cannot wholly destroy. With the utmost desire
to give credit where it is due, and especially to those who
paved the way for us, we claim that we are more careful than
they found it possible to be of the interests of the child, considered not merely or principally as a wage-earner but as a
rational being. Informed that it is a waste of time and energy
and the " ratepayer's " money to try to educate those who
are to be mere day-labourers, teachers refuse to admit the
validity of the argument or the truth of the assertion. No
one, not even the father of a child, has any right to say that
so-and-so was intended to hew wood or draw water, meaning
by these terms some menial work. Every kind of work has
a dignity of its own, redeemed, as it may be, from being
trivial or mean by the spirit and intelligence of the worker.
A man will not be a less efficient crossing-sweeper because he
has received a sound education. He will almost certainly be
a more intelligent voter; receiving due grace, he will without
doubt be a better man from the point of view of real living
if his faculties have been duly trained on the best principles
that research and experience have devised. I hold that
practically every child can be educated, but I wish to avoid
misapprehension and misrepresentation by stating that I use
the word education in the widest possible sense, as the training of all the latent powers and capacities of the individual,
physical, intellectual, emotional, social. The nature and
amount of each department of education to be given to
each individual child will depend on his endowment. Even
those who have most experience of children, with or without
the valuable help that a study of the problems of heredity and
environment gives, will not dogmatise as to what is advisable

or possible for pupils in the mass. They merely insist that the term education be interpreted in its widest sense; that educational considerations should always prevail over extraneous, that the parent, the teacher, the experienced and cautious expert in the application of Intelligence Tests, and the medical man who has made the study of the problems of varying capacity his special care, shall co-operate sympathetically and fearlessly to try to reach a scientific though undogmatic conclusion as to the child's capacity, and that the interests of the child must always be placed first.

There is great need for an advance in the matter of providing classes for the pupils who are greatly above or greatly below the average standard. For these some special provision is urgent and feasible. It is much to be regretted that it is still permissible to herd as many as sixty pupils in a class on the ground of so-called economy. The interests of the pupils demand that the members of the teaching profession, and not they alone, press for a speedy reduction in the size of classes and for the provision of improved and extended facilities for practical hand and eye training in *all* schools.

While improvements in primary school education are doubtless necessary and practicable, these are not revolutionary in their nature. Primary education is on the whole being developed on sound lines which need at most greater breadth, intensity and humanity. Post-Qualifying instruction, however, requires to be envisaged from a new point of view. Far too long it has been carried out on traditional lines. The first and main consideration has been the curriculum, which as a rule has had in view only one type of pupil. Modern conditions of life demand a new orientation with provision of courses carefully planned to suit varying abilities and different outlooks. Luckily the more progressive educators and administrators are agreed on this point, and are making or have already made plans to meet the new situation. But these will not be successful or adequate unless the country can take its courage in both hands and extend the school-leaving age. Up to the present we have been building walls which we leave without roof or coping-stone. Exposed to the elements without protection, the structure not only fails to serve the noble purpose for which it is being built, but it also recalls effort largely baffled and capabilities improvidently unused. Experience proves indubitably that the years from thirteen to fifteen are the most precious and fruitful of the whole period of a pupil's school life—*i.e.*, the school life of a pupil who does not intend to take a full Secondary Course.

The basis of every reasonable course for such pupils must be the study of English widely and generously interpreted, Mathematics, applied Science and Art. In every case, also, there must be very greatly extended facilities for practical work, related as closely as possible to the industries of the district and taught by those who have themselves had experience of the actual conditions of work. Thus a real sense of the dignity of labour will be created. An extension of the school-leaving age to fifteen would remove the fatal and unsettling lure that now attracts boys and girls to leave school at the most critical time of their lives, and thus make possible a consolidation and extension of their previous education with life-long benefits to the individual and incalculable profit to the State.

After the interests of the pupil have been considered, we come naturally to the second part of the Teacher's Charge. It is an essential part of the duty of the profession to promote sound learning. Those who were responsible for the drawing-up of the Charter of the Educational Institute of Scotland were happily inspired in their choice of the word " promote." By using it they showed that they realised the necessity of continual adaptation of means to the securing of ends, and in this respect they were much more far-seeing and showed much more knowledge of real psychology than those who devised the cast-iron Code that was imposed on the schools in the last thirty years of the 19th century. Every institution must justify its existence to its own age. Any one who was unfortunate enough to be educated between 1875 and 1891 knows how essentially unsound were the educational principles and practice of that era. They were in sharp contradiction to the teachings of practical experience and of common-sense.

Taken as a whole, sound learning must be such as will develop all the latent powers of the normal individual. It should fit him for the performance of work and the wise and profitable enjoyment of leisure. It should be such as to develop his reflective, aesthetic and emotional faculties in the interests of noble living. The ideal is admittedly high, but it is not beyond realisation. True, the development may often reach no further than the laying of a foundation on which the pupil himself may build in after life. If teachers begin to compromise with the shibboleths of the time when they are devising courses of sound learning, they will fail in carrying the charge that has been entrusted to them. Sound learning is not fixed and immutable from generation to generation, or even for different individuals in the same age. It is true that what are called the basic subjects, those that underlie the educational structure, are more or less a constant quantity; but the methods of dealing with these must be, and in every progressive system are, subject to modification and improvement in the light of experience day by day. Even the content of the " three R's " is not invariable. A quarter of a century ago, for example, the main stress in the teaching of English was laid on what may be called the analytic study of the subject; modern teachers are more concerned with the appreciative and aesthetic understanding of this, the queen of school studies. Then, the rigid proofs of Euclid were the type and norm of all mathematical study; now, the theory of acceptance has far fewer supporters, and mathematicians are not afraid to construct a Geometry Sequence more in accordance with modern ideas. The battle between the ancients and the moderns which raged so fiercely in the early years of the century has been nearly fought and won. Both sides have come to see that the idea of a rigid, uniform course for all pupils beyond the primary stage is untenable. The demands of our complex modern civilisation necessitate a widening of the horizon. The claims of the advocates of the " new " subjects, such as Science and Drawing, have been conceded. No longer do those who are really interested in the welfare and progress of the country as a whole, claim that the study of foreign languages is an essential ingredient in the development of culture. For a large proportion of pupils the chief means of culture must be the study of the native language and literature, and who will say that the instrument, wisely used by duly qualified teachers conscious of their opportunity and responsibility, is not adequate? Teachers generally rejoice in the broadening of the basis of post-qualifying education, convinced as they are that the freedom now increasingly permitted and encouraged will promote the necessary widening of the curriculum, and make possible the planning and development of more homogeneous Secondary courses. Each of these courses comprising the study of English as a compulsory subject, would, in the later stages at least, permit and even encourage more intensive study of some well-defined combination—Classical, Mathematical, Modern language, or other.

A golden opportunity is presented; it is literally thrusting itself into our hands. If a spirit of earnest desire to co-operate is manifested by ALL who are in any way interested in education, and therefore in the progress of society, it is possible to restore and retain all that is best in the Classical tradition for those who are capable of profiting by Classical study, and at the same time to do justice to essential subjects that were too long proscribed. Moreover, the vexed problem of external examination is in process of being solved for us, although there are some, teachers and others, still bound by tradition. The policy of the permanent heads of the Scottish Education Department in throwing increasing responsibility on those in immediate touch with the pupils is, in my opinion, conspicuously wise. Let teachers justify this generous trust by accepting willingly this honourable addition to their charge, and by using all their influence towards developing really sound Post-Qualifying Courses and making the Certificates real guarantees of ability, application and attainment.

Every system of sound learning postulates the existence of capable teachers. There is no need now to quote the testimony of those best qualified to judge as to the importance of the teacher in the educational economy. The Charter of the Institute expressly provides for guarding the entrance door to the teaching profession in these words :—

> " Also of supplying a defect in the Educational arrangements of that country, by providing for the periodical Session of a Board of Examiners competent to ascertain and certify the qualifications of persons engaged, or desiring to be engaged, in the Education of Youth in that part of our Dominions, and thereby furnishing to the public, and to the Patrons and Superintendents of Schools a guarantee of the acquirements and fitness of teachers for the duties required of them, and thus securing their Efficiency, and raising the Standard of Education in general."

This claim does not seem ever to have been asserted, or if asserted, it was never conceded; but the mere fact that it forms part of the teachers' Commission from the Throne itself shows that their request for Self-Determination is not so extravagant as may appear to the unreflecting. Be that as it may, the teaching profession has always stood for high qualifications and endowments on the part of entrants. Teachers are justified in boasting that without exception they have been foremost in advocating reform and advance in this matter. They supported the abolition of the Pupil Teacher system on humane as well as on educational grounds, just as later on they pressed successfully for the dropping of the Junior Student system, and insisted on the gaining of a Group Leaving Certificate by all candidates for admission to Training Centres. Their resolution stands recorded that there should be a continuous movement towards making a University Degree or its equivalent an essential requirement for recognition as a certificated teacher. Convinced that men and women of the highest culture are required in the schools, they desire that all future teachers should associate on equal terms with aspirants to other professions at the Universities and other seats of learning. Realising the advantages accruing not only to themselves but also to all with whom they are to be brought into contact, they are strongly in favour of post-graduate study at home and abroad, of increasing facilities and opportunities for travel and of Interchange of Teachers between the Mother Country and the Dominions, as well as with foreign nations.

The teaching profession recognises that intellectual ability alone is not a sufficient qualification for the important work of teaching, and the activities of the Institute and its individual members are increasingly devoted to the development of a professional conscience. The Institute's desire is to make its members feel that they are not isolated but united for purposes of mutual help and encouragement, and in order to develop the science and improve the art of education.

These and other laudable and desirable ends cannot be attained without material aids. It is the duty of the united body of teachers to secure that the conditions under which their work is carried on are fair and reasonable. Granting, with reservation perhaps, all that has been said in praise of honest poverty and of the virtues of those, now dead, who toiled without thought of material reward, it is an indisputable fact that the best work cannot be done in any walk of life by those who are haunted by anxiety as to making ends meet. A teacher who is starved physically or intellectually or socially is of necessity a less efficient agent than one whose reasonable wants are satisfied. A discontented profession is a potential danger. At the risk, therefore, of hearing taunts of self-interest, of incurring reproach and even obloquy, it is part of the charge of the profession to endeavour to secure a reasonable standard of comfort for its members, to protect the interests of all its efficient constituents, to advise, guide and succour those who through no fault of their own, or through ill-health, have temporarily or permanently fallen out of the ranks. The teaching profession justly prides itself in being long-suffering and slow to wrath.

In trying thus to fulfil their duties to their fellow-members, teachers are conscious of what they owe to their predecessors who worked under more trying conditions, and they are resolved honourably to discharge this part of their function, one that is not ignoble or despicable, but right and necessary.

There are few words in the language that are more abused than the word Patriotism. It may include the possession and manifestation of the highest virtues. It may, in Dr Johnson's phrase, be the last refuge of a scoundrel. When the State, for the promotion of its own material purposes, proceeds successfully to impose its will on any spiritual institution, the degeneracy of that institution and of the State of which it forms a part is imminent. Germany, in the management of its educational system before the war, is a striking example of such unwarranted interference. The British State, it is true, did prescribe a uniform curriculum for schools during the last thirty years of the nineteenth century, but these conditions have passed away, and teachers will soon be in possession of all the freedom that they are meantime prepared to use. More than ever, therefore, are they becoming free to aid the State in honourable and helpful ways. Opportunities may present themselves of rendering service to the community outside the sphere of school activities. For some minds the call to public life is attractive, and, within limits, such service of the community may be both possible and mutually beneficial. But for the majority of teachers whose capacities are not unlimited, the chief and best service they can render is the faithful performance of their daily task—a service that in their case at least is more an attitude than a conscious striving. Their charge is to educate their pupils in all that is calculated to be immediately and permanently beneficial to them. Teachers need, therefore, to take long views and to be on their guard against the danger of being too busy and leaving no time for reflection. They may sometimes be tempted to consider their sphere narrow and confined, yet they have an almost unrivalled opportunity of guiding and encouraging the footsteps of some who will one day serve the State well or ill according as their instructors have faithfully or unworthily discharged the duty that they have deliberately assumed.

In these times of unrest, which, after all, are not unusual in the long ages of history, and which are better than times of stagnation—fraught as they are with the promise of better things—teachers can do a real service by stressing every day the fact of world interdependence and the increasing need of world neighbourliness. Not wearing " gleaming armour," not having " sharp swords," they may not gain " glittering prizes," but they know a more excellent way, the way of Idealism. " Ideas rule mankind." Let them strive, through the schools, to support and extend a real League of Nations, based on international friendship, justice and goodwill.

THE DEMOCRATIC TRADITION IN SCOTTISH EDUCATION.

THOSE who believe in education for its own sake, and particularly as one of the principal means of maintaining and enhancing our national position, find few deeper causes for regret than the fact that it was found advisable to postpone the coming into force of the clauses of the 1918 Education Act which deal with Continuation Classes. I am well aware of the objections that can be put forward to the idea of compulsory education for young people over fourteen years of age, especially at a time when the economic position of the country is so uncertain, and I admit that the authors and promoters of the Act of 1918 did not foresee all the immediate and more remote difficulties engendered by the aftermath of war. It may even be questioned if those responsible understood clearly how the buildings, equipment, and staffing were to be secured.

That, however, some kind of Continuation Classes are essential if a large proportion of the expenditure on education is not to be wasted, admits of no doubt in the minds of those who have been and are in touch with boys and girls leaving school, and who have the chance of watching their progress, or in many cases, alas, their retrogression, during the three or four years subsequent to their leaving the primary school. The waste that goes on during those most critical years which might be used to such advantage is simply incalculable, and it is, I am firmly convinced, quite avoidable. Many people say they dislike the idea of compulsion, and that it would be from every point of view preferable that Continuation Classes should be conducted on a voluntary basis. It may be at once admitted that the ideal is excellent, but we live in a world where there is often a vast difference between the ideal and the actual, and it is necessary for the country to consider whether it can *afford* any longer to fail to complete the

2

building which it has already spent much time and money in preparing for the roof and coping-stones. More than fifty years ago, while introducing the English Education Act, Mr Lowe declared it was high time that we began to " educate our masters." Since then we have been doing our best to teach them to read, which is an excellent thing, but it is even more necessary, even imperative, that we should teach democracy to think. That can be accomplished only if some kind of regulation or control or guidance is continued through the critical years that lie between the ages of fourteen and eighteen. Superficially, it may seem that there was no definite objective, no clear perception of the goal envisaged by those who first conceived the idea of educating the people and by those who have been responsible for the various advances that have been made towards the realisation of the ideal. As a matter of fact, however, there was method in their zeal, though, as always, some of their contemporaries who were asked to make sacrifices failed to sympathise with their generous enthusiasm. Paradoxical as the statement may seem, it is nevertheless strictly true to say that every step forward in Scottish education has been taken as a result of compulsion.

The question of compulsion is itself worthy of a little consideration and examination. In every community or society, no matter how small, there is no such thing as absolute liberty. That can exist only on an island with one inhabitant, and no civilised person would be envious of such freedom. Compulsion assumes various guises and disguises. There is the compulsion exercised by an autocratic govern- ment, such as that of the Tsars in Russia, where, for its own purposes, and especially the maintenance of absolutism, the ruling class arranged that 90 per cent. of the people should remain illiterate. Such compulsion would, of course, be resisted by many who are themselves almost obsequiously submissive to the compulsion of society and of convention, which is far more dominant over the average individual than the laws of the land would be if these were not backed by an army of officials and the usual deterrents. " What custom wills, in all things should we do it," and many of those who would not face expenditure of time or of money for objects— e.g., education—which are valuable in themselves, are constrained to do so by the compelling influence of what is fashionable or " good form."

There is, again, the compulsion of prudence, in both the better and the less noble sense of that term. Before they undertake any course of action, most people find it necessary to calculate whether it will pay. They will not incur any risk or liability unless they see some tangible advantage, immediate or prospective. Others, usually and rightly considered more magnanimous, consider not only or mainly what will be to their profit, but have regard to the physical, intellectual and social welfare of their family and of their fellow-men. Under this compulsion, motived by a noble prudence, they spend and are spent.

Some, again, act from what may be called the compulsion of benevolence. We have all heard of a benevolent despotism. Half a century ago, and in certain households even at the present time, unquestioning obedience was demanded by the head of the family from every one of his subordinates. The authority was his; the responsibility, too, was his, though it must be said he often took care to bear as few as possible of the unpleasant consequences. But these days have passed or are passing. Nowadays a parent or a government acts in the spirit of benevolence. The compelling motive is the desire to act for the good of the governed though they may not know it or even be able at the time to appreciate the value of what is being done for them. Many of the restrictions laid upon the nations during the war were excused because it was believed that they were imposed in this spirit of benevolence. We should not have tolerated them if our rulers had explained all the grounds for their action, or if we had been able to foresee the daily inconveniences without at the same time being able to understand that they were necessary.

There is also the compulsion that finds its source and justification in the root of democratic government. In this country there can be nothing more foolish or absurd than to speak of having laws passed and imposed upon us against our will. No Government that even attempted to legislate in defiance, or even much in advance, of public opinion, could remain in office for any length of time. We get the Government and, consequently, the laws which we desire and deserve. No doubt we have generous moods—which those who call themselves better balanced, less influenced by madcap notions, are inclined to consider extravagant or even reckless. Under the influence of these emotions we decide upon some fine advance on the less material side of life, and vote for legislators who, we think, can give our ideas concrete form. Or we may have escaped from some imminent danger which had been threatening, but which we, absorbed in more attractive and more profitable pursuits, had treated as non-existent. In the life-and-death fray we had sacrificed our best and bravest, whom we at last recognised we had sent into the jaws of death insufficiently trained and lamentably unprovided with means of defence which our better educated and more scientific, though happily for us more mechanical and brutal, opponents had been preparing for years.

Animated by a noble desire to give the next generation a better chance, the mass of the post-war electors expected that Parliament would act in response to the national feeling and wish as expressed at the election, and naturally welcomed legislation which they felt was essential if future generations were to have a chance of making the most of their powers and opportunities and of keeping abreast of possible competitors and rivals in the material and intellectual spheres. The nation cannot stand still in the matter of education. Having gone so far, we must go farther. We may have to be content for some limited time to depend on the non-compulsory system, but the issues at stake are so momentous that a forward movement cannot be long postponed. Such an advance will be strictly in line with our past history.

Those who advocate the establishment or extension of continued education for pupils beyond the age of fourteen are continually told that it is not the duty of the State to provide instruction beyond the three R's. What the State ought to do may, of course, be a subject for debate; what has been the policy of this country with regard to educational expenditure during the past fifty years is quite obvious. Even in England the conception of elementary education has been immensely widened, until it now includes many kinds of cultural, vocational, and recreative subjects. In Scotland the narrow view of education has never been entertained by those who have been responsible for the nation's government and welfare, and I propose to show that the developments suggested in the years following the war, and already partly initiated, are thoroughly in line with the Scottish educational tradition.

The progress of Scotland in educational matters has been due far more to the foresight of those who founded schools and colleges and Universities largely on a voluntary basis than to any kind of legal compulsion. These patriotic men realised that Scotland was a poor country so far as material wealth was concerned; but they had come to see in their own case and in the lives of others that education was worth having even as a means of securing material success. During the fifteenth century, therefore, they founded no fewer than three Universities in Scotland, and though the University of Glasgow was for a whole century practically a failure, the colleges of St Andrews and Aberdeen were immediately and continuously successful. Owing to the poverty of the country and the selfishness of the nobles, there were at that time no institutions corresponding to modern secondary schools, so the standard of work in the Universities was necessarily very elementary, much inferior to that now prevalent in ordinary higher grade schools. These Universities were really the continuation schools of the time, and as such they did work of inestimable value until, by the establishment of preparatory schools of various grades, they were at liberty to devote themselves to comparatively advanced studies.

It is a remarkable coincidence that the year 1494, which witnessed the foundation of King's College, Aberdeen, is the date of a Statute which ordained that all barons and freeholders should keep their eldest sons at grammar schools until they were " competently founded " and had perfect Latin. There again is the principle of compulsion, for those who did not realise their responsibility. A recent writer gave it as his opinion that probably the greatest name in British—he should have said English—history is that of Oliver Cromwell, and that the larger half of his countrymen hated him and his views and actions. The proportion of Scottish people who do not admire John Knox is not nearly so large, and if we leave out the small minority who can never forgive him for his religious views, there are few who do not admire his conception of having a Latin or grammar school established in every town and an elementary school in every parish. It was in 1560 that Knox enunciated his plan, but not till one hundred and forty years later was an Act passed enforcing the founding of a school in every parish, imposing a tax on the heritors for its upkeep, and placing its supervision in the hands of the clergy. This Act was passed in 1696, which may therefore be looked upon as the date of the beginning of legal compulsion in the matter of education. The central government did not concern itself with education. Each parish was responsible for maintaining and supervising its own schools. The supervision was probably attended to; it is an historical fact that in many parishes the facilities for education were totally inadequate or non-existent. Such was the result when there was no compulsion. Which thing is a warning.

In 1833, Government for the first time gave a grant in aid of education, and this was, of course, followed by Government inspection of schools, the amount of the grant depending on "efficiency" as tested by the passing of an examination by the pupils. Over fifty years ago Scotland received what some consider the doubtful boon of an Education Act which established a School Board in every parish and compelled the levying of a rate for the support of the schools in the parish. Scottish education, which had been under the supervision of the Church from the sixth century, was in 1872 therefore, nominally at least, freed from that supervision, but it is worthy of note that through all these centuries, when there was no legal compulsion to attend school, not only was education not confined to reading, writing, and arithmetic, but the principal stress was laid on Latin and to a minor extent on music instruction, owing chiefly to their being necessary for the intelligent carrying on of religious services. While removing the responsibility for the administration of education from the heritors and minister of each parish, the Act of 1872 respected the Scottish tradition in that it did not, like the English Act of 1870, deal with elementary education alone, but also made provision for the continuation of instruction in Latin and other cultural subjects.

The rise of democracy and the extension of the franchise made it necessary for the State to ensure that the mass of the people were sufficiently educated to enable them to exercise their rights as citizens with some degree of knowledge and intelligence, and in the Act of 1872 and all the succeeding Education Acts down to that of 1918, the Legislature has more and more recognised that education touches life at many points, and it has therefore imposed on those charged with the administration of education many duties and responsibilities that would have been considered entirely outwith their province in the laissez-faire and individualistic years between 1840 and 1865. The detailed story of the gradual widening of the conception of education from 1870 to the present time is exceedingly interesting in itself, and would be enlightening to those who are of opinion that State education has concerned itself only with the three R's. It is not possible at present even to mention all the additional burdens that have been placed upon Education Authorities during the last fifty years, but I shall indicate a few of them in broad outline.

Having taken upon itself, in the interest of the community, the task of compelling children to attend school, the State could not long evade the responsibility of undertaking the whole financial burden by abolishing the payment of fees and of seeing that the children thus brought within the compulsory net were physically fit to receive education. For years, therefore, there has been a compulsory system of medical inspection, in which there are latent great possibilities of good, though unfortunately the duty of providing inspection is not accompanied by the power to compel parents to provide for their children the attention which the medical examination proves to be required. Education Authorities have also important duties and powers in connection with the feeding and clothing of necessitous pupils, of dealing with cases of filth, and diseases and affections of the skin. As prevention is better than cure, Authorities must provide facilities for physical exercises and games, with playing fields and open spaces. It is part of their duty also to find out with regard to mentally defective children whether and to what extent they are educable, to provide for their education, care, and supervision, and to recover from their parents or guardians whatever proportion of the expense they are able to bear. Provision must also be made for securing to epileptics, blind and deaf mutes, whatever education they are capable of receiving. Contributions may be made towards the maintenance of nursery schools for children between the ages of two and five, and of industrial schools where these are necessary.

Reference may be made to a few of the duties and powers that are more closely connected with intellectual training. These include the power to bring opportunities for education within easy reach of children in out-lying districts by conveyance, payment of travelling expenses for teachers or pupils, or of lodgings, and to facilitate attendance at intermediate or secondary schools, University training centres, &c., by payment of travelling expenses, fees, cost of residence in a hostel, bursary or maintenance allowance. In connection with the question of continuation classes, it is important to mention the power to provide any form of education or instruction that may from time to time be sanctioned by any Code or Minute of the Department, and the *duty* to prepare a scheme for the adequate provision of *all forms* of primary, intermediate, and secondary education without payment of fees.

From the day in 563 of our era, when Columba landed in Iona, education became one of the two great objects to whose attainment he and his assistants and successors devoted their energies, and Scottish education from the first had certain features which strongly marked it off from the English conception and practice. In Scotland there has been an intimate connection between the elementary and succeeding grades, maintained largely by the excellence of the parish schools. On the whole, the mass of the people have had higher education much more within their reach than has been the case in England, and the Scottish Universities have been national in the full sense of the term. Few statesmen had such good opportunity as Mr Munro, now Lord Alness, of knowing and understanding the genius and tradition of our educational system. His Act of 1918 was welcomed with practical unanimity as great in conception and rich in promise. He provided an instrument by means of which we may, when we will, by continuation education, consolidate the work already accomplished, and assure a considerable advance in the departments of study which bear more closely on commercial and industrial life.

CHANGING POINTS OF VIEW IN SCOTTISH EDUCATION.

THE years immediately following the war were, so far as Scottish education was concerned, years of hope, anticipation and of some useful planning. The Education (Scotland) Act of 1918 seemed to promise a real advance, if not a revolution in Scottish education. Then suddenly we realised what but for our forgetfulness of the teaching of history we should not have forgotten, that every forward step in the path of progress demands more money, more sacrifice, more effort. Responsive (we educators may think too responsive) to the voice of the people, our rulers decided for rigid, ruthless economy, and for some years we witnessed the effects of retrenchment and stagnation in the educational sphere. Signs of re-awakening are faintly visible. May they speedily become bright and clear!

The 19th century was a time of standardisation in Scottish education. From 1872 up to the closing years of the century the requirements of the various classes were prescribed in the utmost detail. Yearly examination of every pupil in each subject was *de rigueur*. The promotion of the individual pupil depended entirely on his success at this examination, conducted largely by written tests worked in the presence of an examiner who, being virtually a Treasury official, came to look on the child more as a grant-earning machine than as a reasonable being. The effect which this mechanical practice produced on the whole outlook of the schools was immediate and has persisted. The most "liberal" subjects of the curriculum were handled in a mechanical way. Even English was regarded as a grant-earning subject, and studied not with a view to putting the pupil in possession of a key that would unlock the doors leading to the fields of the most splendid and inspiring literature, but to find out as many grammatical and philological difficulties as possible. This theory of "acceptance" was carried to absurd lengths in the study of all the subjects judged worthy of a place in the school course, while several of those subjects that we now think essential found only grudging recognition. In many schools Science, Modern Languages, Art were conspicuous by their absence.

The inevitable result followed. Naturally it began in the Infant School, where the inspiriting influence of reformers like Dr Montessori made itself felt. The centre of gravity was altered. Once again we reverted to first principles. We realised that administration, codes, curricula, tests, &c., are not education; that the child is the centre; that the child must therefore be set in the midst. A genuine and successful endeavour has been made to put first things first, and where reasonable conditions have existed or been provided the result has been surprising. Freedom is the keynote of the modern Infant department, and happiness its prevailing atmosphere. There the idea and the practice of a co-operative commonwealth, with the teacher as a big sister who has not forgotten her dolls, her make-believes, her vanities, have displaced the despotic empire with its prohibitions, its supervisions and its "discipline."

So in the Junior and Senior departments the conception of responsible freedom for the child has triumphed. Reading, writing, arithmetic are still the basic subjects, but the study of these is illustrated, lightened, humanised by concurrent attention devoted to allied subjects. This principle of correlation is carried through the whole of the Primary School course, and it secures due recognition for History, Geography, Nature Study, Drawing, Hand and Eye Training. More and more are the classrooms ceasing to be like workhouses or prisons. Pictures, picture-newspapers, Empire-scenes, gramophones, wireless with all its wonderful accomplishments and possibilities, have worked a revolution in outlook and in practice. Singing, dancing, exercises in the gymnasium and in the open-air, engaged in not at infrequent intervals but literally as the spirit moves, have proved themselves most powerful means of humanistic and sound education. The child that is healthy in body and in mind really loves school. He realises that it is his sphere, that it is indeed a place for work, but that even unavoidable drudgery need not be revolting. It is for him a hive of industry, regulated or rather regulating itself in accordance with the laws that its members are free and glad to observe in the interests of orderly progress.

The most striking change may, however, be noted in post-Primary education. For this stage of education we have various names, such as Higher, Intermediate, Secondary, but in view of the fact that the last two of these terms have come in recent years to have technical meanings referring to certain stages which are now about to disappear, there seems to be a fairly general consensus of opinion in favour of describing all kinds of post-Primary education as Higher.

Scotland is popularly supposed to possess an enviable record in the matter of Higher Education. Comparatively speaking, the claim may be justified. But from 1872 to 1919, even in the most favoured areas, only a moiety of the school population ever reached the secondary stage, and the curriculum could not be said to have regard to conditions and requirements then prevailing. In the course were included very generous quantities of the Latin and Greek classics studied almost entirely from the " dead " point of view with little if any attention to the thoughts, activities and productions of the peoples who spoke these languages. Some attention was devoted to Mathematics, viewed entirely as an abstract body of ascertained facts without reference to the students' immediate surroundings or their possible contacts with scientific development. History was looked upon as a dismal study. Scientific Geography was, as a rule, absolutely neglected. Modern Languages, Science, Drawing, Civics, Singing, Handwork were regarded as " soft options." The introduction of any one of them would have been looked on as betraying the citadel of Secondary education. Most wonderful and most tragical of all, the study of the native Literature found a very humble place, sometimes none at all in the prescribed course. Such was the state of Secondary education in many schools to near the end of the 19th century.

Since that time Higher education in Scotland has been carried on principally in Higher Grade and Secondary Schools. The curriculum of the former must include the study of English with History and Geography, Mathematics, Science and Drawing, together with the study of one or more foreign languages; Secondary School courses must make provision for the study of English with History, Mathematics and foreign languages, and may also provide for other subjects in addition to offering facilities for the study of Music and certain other forms of recreative work.

The changes in the method of study of these higher subjects during the past thirty years have been extraordinary. English study has to a large extent been revolutionised. In what we must, from the point of view of English, describe as the bad old days, the study of English meant in most cases going through one or two prescribed texts in minute detail. Every word was read aloud in class. Meanings were asked, difficult passages were paraphrased, and incidentally emasculated, in "the pupil's own words." Analysis and parsing were reduced to a precise science. Everything that could be conceived was done to destroy the pupil's interest and to make him hate the very word English. His knowledge of "Literature" was derived from a compendium with lists of authors, writings and dates. School libraries did not exist. The time devoted to "English" was naturally looked upon as wasted. But in all but a negligible fraction of schools a real transformation has been wrought. Every school has its library; most English class-rooms have collections of books which are open to the pupils at all times. During the five or six years of the Secondary Course the pupil is introduced to a considerable number of the best books in each of the great departments of English literature. Appreciation is now the mot d'ordre. From being the Cinderella English has become the queen of school subjects. Many of the pupils are the proud possessors of small libraries, chosen and acquired on the only sound principle—that of individual taste and appreciation. Teachers have learned that their function in English instruction is to inspire and introduce, not to direct, much less to impose.

History and Geography must, in the Primary school at least, continue to be taught in close conjunction with English. It cannot be reasonably claimed that these subjects are as effectively taught in Scottish schools as they might be. Teachers are still too much obsessed with the idea that there must be a definite, prescribed "dose" of History and Geography for each class with little if any reference to

previous or subsequent study of these subjects or to their
relation to other parts of the curriculum. But the waters are
being stirred. Much more of the human element is being
introduced. History is treated not as a series of detailed
incidents, but as the record of the lives of actual men, women
and children, their houses and their dress, their work and
their play. What may be called the picturesque element is
in the foreground. The past is made to live as the essential
means of understanding the present. And the horizon is
widening. Brave and noble deeds on the part of our kinsfolk
across the seas and of our allies arouse the sense of wonder
and of interest, and our pupils are becoming more truly
patriotic because they are being trained to be less insular.
Pride in being citizens of a great empire is not incompatible
with a deep conviction that on the application of the principles
of the League of Nations any reasonable hope of solid
progress must be based. Geography is being treated on more
scientific lines than formerly. Much credit for this more
rational conception is due to those who have made available
for the use of schools improved equipment in the way of
pictures; charts; illustrations in books; atlases physical,
political, ethnographical. The daily newspaper and other
more or less popular periodicals are being utilised as helps
in Geographical teaching, especially in its commercial and
intellectual relationships.

Latin and Greek study is also now conducted on modern
lines. By means of pictures, talks and similar aids, the pupil
is from the first made to feel that these languages are not
" dead." The labour of learning declensions and conjuga-
tions is not evaded, but it is lightened by the introduction
from the very first lesson of what may be called the human
element. In my own school we begin reading simple Latin,
illustrated by pictures, as part of the first lesson, and the
immediate and sustained interest of the pupils proves that
the method is both natural and wise.

The French and German languages have since their introduction to Scottish Schools nearly always been studied on
more reasonable lines, but the pupils' interest and enthusiasm
have been considerably enhanced and developed in recent
years by taking advantage of the facilities that now exist for
foreign correspondence, of the gramophone, of talks by wire-

less, &c. Acknowledgment should be made of the enterprise shown by the publishers of cheap literature in the form of books, magazines and newspapers.

Space does not permit of attempting to deal with the new conceptions and methods devised and applied to the teaching of Mathematics, Science, Drawing and Handwork. In Mathematics the shackles of Euclid's fixed system have been broken in favour of a modern Geometrical sequence.

Science teachers have come to realise that the systematising motive has been unduly stressed, and are preparing courses in which the wonder motive will receive much greater prominence. The study of Art has ceased to be mere imitation, and now concerns itself with everything that cultivates the aesthetic side of the pupil's nature.

In reviewing the history of Scottish education during the twentieth century one finds much solid ground for believing that sound progress has been made. Education has become increasingly paidocentric. Teachers are giving close study to the problems and teaching of child psychology. As a people we are becoming less insular and more tolerant, though not less proud of our inheritance as members of the Empire. The teaching profession in Scotland is keen on educational advance.

For all pupils under the age of seventeen external examinations by the Department ceased to exist in 1924. On teachers is thrown the main responsibility of planning courses and testing progress. When our rulers provide the necessary facilities for an advance, Scotland's educational army is ready to move forward in the van.

SUBJECTS OF INSTRUCTION.

INTELLIGENT interest in educational problems on the part of the ordinary layman has always been an admirable feature in the life of progressive nations. Even the spirit of criticism, so long as it arises from praiseworthy motives, is valuable as indicating a desire for progress, and remembering that the man who pays for the music should have some voice in calling the tune, those more immediately concerned with the practical work of education will always welcome any reasonable suggestions towards securing that the best possible use is being made of the available means. Some individuals and certain organised bodies advance objections such as the following to the present system of education. The curriculum is overloaded. Insufficient time and attention are given to reading, writing, and arithmetic. Useless subjects are taught, and time and money are wasted on subjects that unfit the pupil for his future work. Pupils leave school with a distaste for manual work. They are not so adaptable or reliable as they were a generation ago. There should be a scrapping of all new-fangled methods and subjects, and concentration on what will really benefit the pupil in earning his living.

Now it may be admitted that in recent years there has been a tendency in some schools to give too much time to what the man in the street calls " fads," but not a single one of these was introduced except at the direct command of the Scottish Education Department, which, having the power of the purse and a staff of inspectors to see that each new subject received a " due " share of attention, was able to dictate the policy. Many of those who now criticise never uttered a word of protest when the Department insisted on the introduction of subjects of doubtful value, and there was a general scramble to get a share of the extra grants offered on apparently tempting conditions.

A considerable amount of recent criticism has been made in evident forgetfulness of certain rather important considerations. Thirty years ago only a very small proportion of pupils remained at school till they were fourteen or fifteen years of age. The large majority, in country districts at any rate, had taken the labour certificate, and thus gained exemption from further attendance at school, at the age of twelve, eleven, or even ten. The brighter the pupil, the earlier he could leave by attaining the necessary standard of education. The consequence was that only a few of those whose parents were better-off stayed at school and fitted themselves for office and similar work. The modern conception of education is much wider than that of a generation ago. One cannot imagine a system of primary education which would not be based on reading, writing and arithmetic, and these subjects will always receive by far the major part of time and attention, but there are other subjects, which are not only not harmful to the study of these basic subjects, but which tend greatly to promote the successful pursuit of them.

Any subject which rouses the interest of the pupil, which broadens his outlook and, therefore, develops his intelligence, which increases his capacity for appreciating the value and the beauty of the realms of Nature and imagination has a claim to receive some attention. Moreover, we must remember that the hours of leisure are from the social and moral points of view of first-rate importance, and in school arrangements and work we can neglect some preparation for the wise use of these hours only with great peril. Normal children have to be taught concentration as they have to be taught every other habit, even speaking the truth. Valuable as the three R's may be, they must be supplemented and lightened by reasonable variety of occupation. Children cannot read, write, and count all the time. These subjects will not, unaided, help greatly to train little hands or eyes or ears, all of which need early and systematic training. The school of a former age was too much of a prison from which the pupil was glad to escape. It did little to create and develop and maintain interest. Those whose experience of the conditions of school life and work dates from, say, thirty years ago, should visit a well-equipped, well-taught infant or junior department. They will find that the pupils are not only quite as intelligent as those of a former age, but keenly interested in many things and subjects which were strictly excluded then.

We need to remember that there are two main conceptions of what education should aim at. Some hold that it should be largely if not entirely vocational—what has been called a "bread-and-butter" education, keeping in view only or chiefly what will be immediately useful to the pupil when he leaves school. Others maintain that the main objective should be the training of the various powers and faculties of the child without direct consideration of his possible future occupation. The advocates of the former kind of " preparation for life " are not agreed among themselves. They tell us that the " practical " subjects taught in schools are in reality a hindrance rather than a help in after life. Moreover, the demand that education should be confined to such studies as will bear directly on the future work of each pupil is manifestly absurd when it is recalled that teachers have to teach as many as sixty pupils in one class, or forty to fifty and over in two or three classes simultaneously. Primary school education must therefore have for its principal aim the development of the powers of the average pupil, the putting him in possession of a key which will enable him to enter one of the various realms of service and of interest that may be within his reach. It must, to use a rather hackneyed word, be cultural. Teach a boy to think for himself, and you need not trouble as to whether he will be able to adapt himself to circumstances.

The point I have been trying to make is well brought out by a Commission on the teaching of English in the following words:—" There are two delusions about the education of the people; it is difficult to say which is the more mischievous. There is the delusion, still sometimes surviving, that the only education which they ought to have is that which trains their hands to the plough or their eyes to the needle, which has exclusively in view the making of miners or factory girls, engineers or cooks. That is the educational ' lie in the soul ' whether it comes from the selfishness of those who wish to employ, or the shortsightedness of those who wish for employment. The other delusion is not that manual labour unfits a man for education, but that education makes him too good for manual labour. Both the idea that the man

3

who works with his hands ought not to have a humane education, and the idea that when he has got one he cannot continue to work with his hands, grow out of the idea that education is exclusively an affair of vocation. The first thought of education must be fulness of life, not professional success. That is the only universal educational ideal." Those who were brought up on the method of education with which the average pupil had to be satisfied forty years ago must admit that it was grievously deficient from the points of view of social life and of the wise and profitable spending of the valuable yet critical hours of leisure.

PRIMARY SCHOOL CURRICULUM.

IS the curriculum of the primary school overloaded? The question has been so often asked and answered, generally in the affirmative, by those who declare that the former days were better than the present, that many people are inclined to agree who do not wish to go to the trouble of inquiring. Generally speaking, the curriculum of the primary school is not overloaded, but so many people have been tinkering at it and trying experiments, that the time has come when a reconsideration of value is imperative.

The principal fault in connection with the primary curriculum at present arises from the failure on the part of teachers and others who draw up schemes of work to keep clearly in view the essential difference between basic and subsidiary subjects. Another fault, almost equally serious, springs from failure to co-ordinate the subjects of instruction. Those are in the right who demand that the three R's should get the principal share of attention, but it is necessary to define the terms we use. Learning to read printed matter is largely a mechanical process, and if modern methods are adopted, as they are in an overwhelming proportion of schools, the average pupil can at the age of nine read much more fluently than the average pupil of twelve could do some twenty years ago. And he not only can, but does. The understanding and appreciation of literature is, however, a very different pursuit. That is something which requires careful planning and assiduous application on the part of all concerned. English literature is the finest in the ancient or the modern world both in range and in quality. No reading-book selections can give any fair estimate of its value, and I trust the time is not far distant when, as supplementary to class reading, we shall see pupils engaged in the study of real literature without notes or abridgment. To attain this end the Carnegie Trust and Education Authorities must combine their resources and energies to provide an abundant supply of library books for every class of every school. The important thing to remember in connection with pupils' reading is to give them heaps and heaps of material. And in connection with reading there must be the study of history and geography and nature, looked upon, not as separate subjects each in its own water-tight compartment, but as complementary to English study and as affording unlimited material for creating and widening interest, and thus of supplying stores of information and topics for oral and written expression. History teaching can no longer deal only with our own island. Whether we like it or not, we are concerned with the affairs of the whole world, as the whole world concerns itself with ours, and having extended the franchise so that practically every adult has the same voice as his neighbour in directing the destinies of the world, we must educate our masters in school or suffer the penalty of our neglect. And the plea for the scientific treatment of geography is equally cogent. We hear objections to the proposed introduction of the teaching of Civics, and I admit that the word suggests something rather indefinite and even enigmatic, but only a little knowledge of the first principles of government might help to keep potential and actual voters from swallowing the nostrums of the political quack-doctor. These subjects are all so intimately connected that in the primary school they should be closely grouped, and in reality form only one subject.

If the charge is well-founded that pupils cannot count well, the man in the street, or rather the employer, has good ground for complaint. Arithmetic has always been considered one of the best means of cultivating the reasoning powers, and in my opinion it holds a position second only to that of English as a means of preparation for the actual business of life. It is, of course, possible to over-estimate its importance from the point of view of earning one's living, because a very small percentage of people have in the course of their daily lives to perform more than the simplest calculations. Schools have undoubtedly been guilty of a radical mistake in connection with the teaching of arithmetic when they have forgotten that people in ordinary life do not carry a slate by their side. There are "ready reckoners" and similar aids for those who are engaged in ordinary business and in the realms of high finance. Pupils in school should have their energies devoted to simple rules and examples in calculations. An important feature in every department of life and, therefore, of education, which it is rightly claimed should, in part at least, be a preparation for life, is that every step should be taken after due reflection; hence the reasoning is as important as getting the correct result. Remembering this, I have no hesitation in saying that the study of science should, in the upper classes of the primary school, be an integral part of the work in calculation. It will afford both interest and material for manipulation.

As in the case of reading, looked upon from the point of view of knowing the words, writing is largely mechanical, and in these days of typewriters may be considered by some as of little importance, but there are still many departments of business life where good handwriting is an asset of great value, and it may be questioned whether the average pupil who leaves school at fourteen years of age is as neat in his handwriting as his predecessor. Ability to express one's ideas correctly, idiomatically, and intelligently is of the first importance. No amount of mere writing will, however, secure much proficiency in this art. Here, writing must be in close conjunction with the study of literature and of language. Appreciation and imitation of the best writers, combined with patient analysis, are the only roads to success.

In every well-regulated primary school quite three-fourths of the time is given to the above-mentioned basic subjects, which are to be regarded as closely related and of first-rate importance. There are a few subsidiary subjects such as drawing, music, physical exercises, and such practical work as cookery or wood-work. The time devoted to these amounts in the aggregate to some four or five hours weekly, except in the very rare instance where some " expert " has been able to filch an undue proportion of school time. If these subjects are kept in their place, I hold, and have proved by experience, that due attention to them, with first-rate teaching, will not only not delay progress in basic subjects, but will improve the quality of all school work. They rouse and maintain a lively interest, which is half the battle in education, and which is very often—e.g., in the case of music, art, &c.—

continued and increased after school days. To be trained for the hours when he must be busy at his daily occupation is excellent; to have tastes and desires and emotions cultivated that will help to make the adolescent a good social animal and enable him to spend rationally his leisure time is probably quite as necessary for fulness of life. " Education is preparation for life not merely for livelihood; and any school activity that contributes to the amenities of existence and intercourse is a necessary and laudable part of the educational system."

Reasonable criticism of education and educational methods is always to be welcomed, because in this, as in many other spheres, to stand still is to stagnate; but we have to discriminate between the critic who desires to see progress and the " economist " who grudges all expenditure that does not bring in an immediate, tangible result. The education that was reasonably satisfactory when a mere fraction of the people was in attendance at school will not be sufficient to meet the needs of a more complex age. There is no greater danger to a country than to put power into the hands of an uneducated democracy, and the process of teaching to think is long and laborious. " A democracy which has only learned to read, without learning to weigh and to discriminate, is a much greater danger to the world than its illiterate ancestors, for it is much more liable to be misled. Without judgment, the man follows his favourite newspaper, blindly, hoping all things, believing all things "—(Bryce). The times change. We must change with them, and with judgment adapt our subjects and methods of instruction to the needs of the age.

ENGLISH, THE QUEEN OF SCHOOL SUBJECTS.

ONE of the most interesting and hopeful features in discussions of educational problems is the general recognition of the importance of the place of English among the subjects of instruction. It is true, of course, that there is the usual conflict of opinion between those who think that education should concern itself chiefly, if not entirely, with such subjects as will contribute directly to making the pupil a better worker and those who take a wider view of the duties and responsibilities of the school. All, however, who give any consideration to the matter, are agreed that "Reading" is of primary importance, and those who remember that the large majority of pupils will never have any chance of being introduced to another language as a means of culture will insist that, if possible, even greater attention be given to English in the future than in the past.

It has been well said that the three main motives that influence the human spirit are the love of goodness, the love of truth and the love of beauty. These qualities are not native. They need to be carefully cultivated and developed, and every subject that will in any way help to promote the attainment of this end should be included in a sound educational programme. Dealing as it does with human motive, human character and human action, literature is an admirable agent for the development of the intelligence and the imagination. Literature must never be regarded as a kind of ornament, something that may be useful as a kind of pastime to be taken up or laid down at will, something that is a mere "accomplishment," as an earlier generation regarded calisthenics. Nothing will make up for neglect of early attention to education in English. It is unique in this sense, that the pupil can make no progress whatever in any other branch of study until he has acquired a certain command of his own language. Defects in connection with the learning of other subjects, such as arithmetic, history, civics, may be remedied later, but one who lacks language is devoid of a means of communication with his fellow-men and even of the power of thought itself. English is, therefore, not merely one among many branches of education. It is the essential foundation and preliminary. Without it there can be no super-structure.

To teachers in particular does this apply. In proportion as their knowledge of English is deep or superficial, so will their teaching of every other subject be effective or unsatisfactory. Their own future progress in culture and worth to pupils and community will be determined largely by their acquirements in their native language and literature. The teacher who can enthuse pupils by vivid presentation of the subject in hand has usually found the key of his inspiration in devotion to English literature and language. One who does not read—in a real sense—is absolutely disqualifying himself for being a teacher of any subject. The poverty of the country in which he lives, the scantiness of the fare on which he tries to eke out a miserable, hypocritical existence intellectually, will soon be evident to the meanest intelligence. Every teacher worth his salt is, and must continue to be, a student of his own subject, but he must also cultivate and maintain and develop a love for English literature in as many of its branches as possible. The most lasting, because the deepest, impressions are those that we make unconsciously. If our own minds and hearts have been inspired by devotion to even a few masterpieces of literature, some answering note will certainly be stirred in the eagerly responsive souls of those with whom, as teachers, we are brought into such intimate touch. I have been told by the very distinguished Master of a Cambridge College that he and his fellow-pupils in a rural school in Aberdeenshire received their first insight into the glories of English literature, and far more than the beginnings of any power of appreciating it that they possessed, from the reading to them as a special treat of choice passages selected by their over-worked schoolmaster, who struggled with all classes from infants to bearded young men about to enter the University.

It is perhaps necessary to recall that the study of English in schools and colleges implies two things—the study of language and the study of literature. These two departments have often been combined, and I am convinced that the attempt to teach language and literature in the same breath, so to speak, is a mistake. I believe that the custom has persisted from the time when English education was based on the study of Latin and Greek. In what are called the public schools of England, much more time is still devoted to the study of the classical languages than is given to English, and some forty or fifty years ago Latin and Greek were the staple pabulum of the few pupils in Scotland who were educated beyond the elementary stage. They were taught the classical tongues every day, and practically all day. English as such received little attention except in the way of parsing and analysis, and the method that was almost inevitable in dealing with a highly inflected language like Latin was continued when more attention came to be given to the study of the native language. Of course, we must not forget that the study of English is one of the finest means of mental training and discipline, and that it is essential that the student be trained to habits of accurate observation and to acquire the power of understanding even the most abstruse arguments and reflections of such writers as Bacon and Burke. For that purpose the work of analysis, derivation, criticism, comparison, interpretation, and précis-writing must be carried on with increasing intensity from the early to the highest stages. But there are abundant materials for such essential analytic work without practising on the fine flowers of English literature. There are those, it is said, who would botanise on their parents' grave. Doubtless they are of this breed who would set a class to parse the verbs in, say, " The Lost Leader " or the ninetieth psalm. Language-teaching and literature study should be, therefore, kept from conflicting. They are antipathetic.

From several points of view it is desirable that a reasonable proportion of the young people of Scotland should be introduced to the wonderful literatures of Greece and Rome if they have the capacity and inclination for classical work. But regret on this score is considerably lessened by the reflection that English literature is one of the finest and, looked at from the points of view of range, quality and content, practically the richest in the world. Like some majestic river, it has received tributaries from the literatures of every land. And all the contributions from the various sources have been so transmitted by the genius of our great writers that the resultant product is in truth original and spontaneous. In this unique pageant we find a wealth of material to suit all ages and most tastes. Among many other evils for which the Great War, or the unregulated passions that let loose the dogs of war, must be held responsible, none is more to be regretted from the educator's point of view than the enormous increase in the price of books, but it is very false personal or national economy that tries to save on the books necessary for introducing the rising generation to the glories of English literature, with its folk-tales and songs, its fables and parables, its myths and legends, its romance and adventure, its history and biography, its lyrics, its epics, its dramas, and its unparalleled wealth of great works dealing with every phase of human emotion, endeavour and action.

Asked as to the uses of great men, Carlyle replied in his usual gruff manner to those who asked irrelevant questions, " Uses? We will not estimate the sun by the quantity of gaslight it saves us." Every subject of school instruction well taught has its own value, but literature is something unique, permanent, independent of time and place. Literature is the only University that is within the reach of most of us, and we neither need nor deserve commiseration when the substitute is so satisfactory. It is a means of uniting all classes without distinction of birth, social condition, or employment. The love of literature is a permanent possession that is capable of bringing, and does bring to all who have become its devotees, means of refreshment, instruction, and delight. " Its object," Wordsworth tells us, " is truth, not individual and local, but general and operative; not standing upon external testimony, but carried alive into the heart with passion."

And the attainment of these seemingly lofty heights is by no means difficult for those who will expend the necessary time and money and effort. There are hundreds of schools where the study of English literature is a delight. What is needed is to demand a much higher standard in this subject from entrants to the Universities and Training Centres, that all the English study at these institutions be co-ordinated and systematised, and that every teacher of every school subject should have taken English classes at least up to the standard of the M.A. degree.

The pupil may, and probably will, forget much that he has learned with painful effort. If, however, he has been imbued with a love for literature, he will have abiding cause to be grateful to those who introduced him to such an inexhaustible store of delight. The task of the teacher in trying to lead his pupils to real personal appreciation of literature is hard indeed; there is no part of his work that is more fascinating or more richly rewarded.

The attempt to place the pupil in such a position that he will gradually acquire the power of appreciating to some extent what is admirable, and of retaining his taste for work of a high quality in English prose and verse, must therefore, I think, be the teacher's first and main concern, but it must certainly not be his only objective. Analytic work must go side by side with the appreciative, and that consideration brings us right against the question as to whether the study of English alone is sufficient as a means of training the intellectual powers. Can a pupil derive from his English studies the mental training and discipline which are supposed to be the special prerogative of the study of foreign languages, especially Latin and Greek?

In the case of pupils who are looking forward to any of what are called the learned professions, and especially for future teachers, the importance of the study of foreign language can hardly be too much stressed, and, if conditions were ideal, it might be reasonable to require that the great majority of those who are in the upper departments of schools should study at least one language in addition to their own. In present circumstances, however, such a proposal is merely a counsel of perfection. Experience proves that even of those who begin the study of Latin or French, only a minority go far enough to enable them to derive solid benefit. If pupils are confined to formal grammar for the first year, or even two years, of their foreign language study, as is still unfortunately the case in too many instances, those of them whose school life is short have hardly time to begin to appreciate the literature or even to see what immediate or prospective benefit will accrue. Even in schools where language study is carried out on reasonable lines, necessity or choice depletes the classes of much too great a proportion of those who began with fair promise of success. Such a result, though in every way regrettable, need not make us despair. English study alone can be made an efficient means of culture. Everything depends on the method. No matter how potentially powerful a subject may be, if it is studied in an unscientific way the result will be unsatisfactory. On the other hand, any subject of study scientifically handled will produce its due effects.

At first sight, indeed, English as a subject of study seems to have a great advantage over Latin or French. It is sometimes asserted that as English is their native language pupils can understand from the first, and therefore make much more progress. Unfortunately, the assumption is not warranted. In many parts of the country, and in too many occupations, English is in reality a foreign language. If any one questions this, let him listen to the conversation of any company on a sports field, or read a batch of " English " compositions. In many cases there is so much to unlearn, and such a powerful social force acting in a direction opposed to that of the school teaching of English that it almost seems more promising to teach successfully a language that is foreign in name as well as in fact.

Generally speaking, it seems difficult to get from the study of English alone the intellectual benefit that may be derived from the systematic study of an additional language. In any case, it cannot be said that success has been secured by the methods hitherto in use. It may be that these have followed too slavishly the Latin and Greek models. It is many years since Ruskin showed how a scientific study could be carried out of such a classical work as Milton's *Lycidas* without any first-hand knowledge of classical phraseology or mythology, and a really strenuous attempt must be made to devise suitable courses and methods of study for those who cannot hope to learn any foreign tongue. An essential condition of success is the provision of facilities for study at least as extensive as are supplied for other departments of school activity. The best and most up-to-date dictionaries, encyclopædias, historical and geographical atlases, source-books, are indispensable. The Universities and Training Centres must provide an abundant and increasing supply of thoroughly qualified and capable teachers, not mere intellectuals who vapour and rhapsodise and patronise, but ordinary work-a-day beings with at least a few human frailties and willing to approach the stern task of teaching English with the same devotion and scientific accuracy as are necessary for success in the teaching of other subjects.

Such a training in appreciation and understanding as has been outlined must be judged, to some extent at least, by its results, and that there is some dissatisfaction with these at present is undoubted. It is true that the value to be allowed to any criticism must depend to some extent on the point of view and the personal interest of the critic, and it is quite likely that there may be a more or less unconscious bias in the estimate of, say, the business man or the farmer who feels inclined to censure the product of the modern school. In too many cases these critics concern themselves less with their young apprentice's grounding for life and living than with the extent of his immediate usefulness to themselves. They make unthinking and unreasonable demands on the schools for some kind of vocational training or for an amount of knowledge not to be expected at the time when the average pupil leaves a school in which are massed pupils of very different capacity and destined for the most varied occupations. It is, and always must be, impossible for the ordinary school, whether primary or secondary, to supply " perfect " workmen. If pupils on leaving school have begun to form habits of industry, reasonable accuracy and adaptability, if they have learned to read in such a way as increasingly to train their imagination, to use books as suggestions for ideas and as means of testing, supplementing and applying the experiences that come to them in the course of their business and social life, the schools are not deserving of censure. In any case, the most successful modern business firms are agreed that they find most useful to them the boy who has received a broad-based training not conceived on vocational lines. Fortunately the training that is most conducive to success in business life—namely, intensive study of English in its various aspects, linked up increasingly with the study of history— is also the best discipline for ensuring general culture. Let us have as much education in other branches as circumstances will allow. We cannot devote too much time and energy to the study of English.

SINGING IN SCHOOLS—FROM THE NON-SPECIALIST POINT OF VIEW.

A STRIKING phenomenon in connection with education is the fact that every now and then special stress is laid on some department or branch of school work to which attention is particularly called as if it were something new. Circulars emphasising the importance of devoting a certain amount of time to the fashionable craze or " fad " are apt to mislead the inexperienced or the unwary. There is danger that the curriculum may be overcrowded if the distinction between basic and subsidiary subjects is forgotten owing to the putting forward of demands that an unreasonable amount of time be devoted to comparatively unimportant subjects. There is also a tendency on the part of young teachers to keep subjects, and even departments of subjects, in water-tight compartments, and this tendency is apt to become exceedingly pronounced if the " specialist " element is allowed to become too prominent in primary education. In the interests of a sound, well-balanced curriculum, this proclivity should be carefully restrained. There is hardly any department of school work that cannot be brought into close relation with the study of English and Arithmetic.

I have elsewhere shown how his can be done in connection with Drawing, and I wish to attempt to show that the same is possible in the case of Singing. There will inevitably be a reaction against these subjects if they are allowed to usurp a position of undue importance, and as I consider that they have both an immediate and a permanent value as subjects of study, and therefore believe that it would be a calamity if they were crowded out owing to the misplaced zeal of enthusiasts in demanding what is impracticable, I make a plea for tempering zeal with discretion.

Much has recently been spoken and written about music and its appreciation, about Directors of Music, and of the need for starting on new lines because the old methods were bad. It has to be admitted that teachers, like other people, are apt to get into grooves, but great harm is done to the study of any subject by the unbalanced enthusiast who insinuates that wisdom appeared in the world only when the enthusiast himself appeared. There were brave men before Agamemnon, and there were capable teachers of singing, many of them teachers of all the other class subjects, before the days of specialists. It is thoroughly advisable that the best teachers should be secured for every subject, but, except in large centres, it is impossible on the ground of economy to have specialists for every branch, and I am by no means certain that the visiting teacher, however highly qualified, always produces better work than the ordinary class teachers who, with it may be fewer natural gifts in a certain department, have more breadth of outlook and the advantage of being always with the pupils, and therefore in a position to co-ordinate the whole of the school work and to enliven the dull hours of school work by occasional relief in the form of a song, or a tale, or even a dance.

Those who are interested in the development of music-teaching in school should consider what is possible and what is practicable. If a due proportion is to be preserved among subjects, one hour a week is all that can be devoted to singing in ordinary schools. In no subject, perhaps, is it more necessary theoretically that individual tuition should be the rule, but such attention cannot possibly be given in schools where the classes are large.

I hold that, as in the case of Drawing, every *normal* child is musical. By that I do not mean that he has a good ear for music, though it has been proved that the ear can be trained if the pupil is caught early enough. Owing to his circumstances or environment a pupil may never have had music presented to him in the proper way, but every normal child has the instinctive desire for self-expression in music. Just as children are unable to express themselves intelligibly until they have learned the use of words, so we must first learn the language of music and then use it as the means of bringing out the musical feeling that is in us.

Those who begin the teaching of singing with the notes are undoubtedly making a mistake. Following the usual method of teaching a child to speak, we should begin by making the pupil listen to music, not note by note, but in whole sentences and stanzas. Listening comes first; expression follows, and if the child's craving for language, whether of speech or of music, is stirred, he will endeavour to express himself. As in drawing, where conventional methods which destroyed all initiative and denied to the pupil the opportunity of realising himself have given place to the more rational principles of recent times and especially the methods of Professor Cizek, so in music the analytic method must, in the earlier stages at least, yield to that of cultivating the innate powers in the natural way. In the teaching of modern languages this principle of laying more stress at the early stage on the genius and less on the dry bones is being adopted with increasing success. Children who are brought up in musical homes are nearly always musical. For those who have not this privilege, we must endeavour to produce musical surroundings and facilities.

If it be true that the hearing of music is essential to the pupil's learning to sing, steps must be taken to let him hear much music. The piano is not a very suitable instrument for this purpose, as it has an idiom of its own. Recourse is being had more and more to the gramophone, notwithstanding strenuous opposition in certain circles to its use on the ground that it is a " mechanical contrivance," a limitation which, of course, it shares with the piano. It has this great advantage over the piano, that if the records are good—it is understood, of course, that a school gramophone will not be cheap and nasty—it gives a more or less faithful interpretation of the ideas of the composer, and that there is no limit to the selections that it can produce. If the accompaniment is played on the piano by the class teacher, she cannot give the same attention to the pupils as is possible when the gramophone is employed. However well the class-singing is taught, and no matter how proficient the pupils may become, the children do not hear singing, so as to appreciate it, when they themselves are performing.

I take it that musical appreciation means simply the power of listening to music in such a way as to understand what the composer's ideas were, and this power can be developed only by listening. Even in towns it is not by any means practicable to take the mass of children to hear good concerts; in country districts it is impossible. But the gramophone brings real music within the reach of all. There is no limit to the scope or the variety of the tunes that the gramophone plays, and the current expenses are small after the initial outlays have been met. The day cannot surely be far distant when every school in which a modern language is taught shall have a really good gramophone, which could be used for several departments of school work—*e.g.*, language teaching, singing and elocution. If it is for any reason impossible to secure a good gramophone as an aid in cultivating the ear, it is usually possible to fall back on the fiddle or the penny whistle, or even whistling without a whistle if the powers that be destroy the wee herd's home-made one. Any one of these will help to develop the pupil's ear and enable him to " appreciate music."

The question as to which notation should be used in the teaching of singing in schools has lately been receiving much attention. Theoretically, there is no doubt that the advantages are almost wholly with the staff notation, because once learned it needs no supplementing or modification to enable the student to learn to play any instrument to which he may have the inclination or the need to give attention. Thirty or forty years ago, when scant consideration was given in the majority of schools to singing, the larger number of those who wished to learn were advised to take the tonic sol-fa method, and the advice was sound, for it is undoubtedly easier, especially for adult beginners. The staff notation, like the multiplication table, needs to be learned when one is young.

But for the last three decades at least the teaching of singing has been compulsory in every school—it was a terrible trial to the University graduate, who had no " polite accomplishments " to get his pupils ready for H.M.I.'s tests in singing—and though the time available, one hour per week, is not very large, a good deal can be accomplished. In the nine years of his primary school life the pupil would receive some three hundred and sixty hours instruction, and in that time every child of average capacity should have learned enough to be able at the age of fourteen to read a simple melody at sight. To make this possible, the work must be

4

carefully graduated and sedulously prosecuted with a view to
the pupil's not only comprehending, but also enjoying the
lessons. It is true that music is from some points of view
a recreative subject, but that does not imply that the goal
should be at all less definite or less often reached than is
the case in the teaching of literature or any other subject.

The singing lesson should not be regarded merely as a
pastime, though, in junior classes at least, it is advisable that
the lighter or recreative side should be fairly prominent. The
objective to be kept in view during the eight or nine years of
primary education in singing may be summarised under the
heads of ear-training, voice-production, training and development of the sense of rhythm and the practice of songs, but
it is essential that the wider aim should be continually
emphasised—namely, that the pupil may be able to understand, appreciate and enjoy. Only if this result has been to
some extent attained can the spending of time and effort on
singing be justified.

Music has one great advantage over several other school
subjects. Complaints are frequently heard that young people
forget the larger part of what they learned at school, that
their ability to work even simple problems wanes, that they
forget how to make out an account, that even their interest
in reading and in literature fades, and it must be admitted that
in many cases there is truth in the charge. But neither the
system nor the instructor is necessarily at fault, for in the
first place the vast majority of pupils leave school before their
education has been consolidated and when they are at a restless age, and in the second place many of them have little
or no opportunity of practising and keeping up what they
have learned. In the matter of singing the case is entirely
different. Almost every church choir is ready to welcome
qualified or even promising recruits. Much of the pleasure
of family and social life is created by those who have the
education and the will to contribute their quota to the entertainment and instruction of others. Those who have learned
either notation thoroughly at school can render valuable
service to the community in connection with concerts, guilds,
and similar institutions. I have no belief in the system of
entertaining people in a spirit of condescension; it is little
better than patronage for which the patrons often deserve

and generally receive scanty thanks or credit. But that people of all ages should help by their talents to brighten the hours of leisure is very desirable, and there is probably no one who can contribute more to this result than the trained singer.

There is another substantial reason for devoting a definite though limited amount of time to singing in schools. As I have already indicated, a training in singing is one of the best means of producing a sensitive ear, which is so valuable in many kinds of scientific work and in most departments of practical life. Moreover, the training of the ear postulates the training of the mind which is behind the ear. Clearness of enunciation is not merely pleasing, it is of very considerable importance in all kinds of professional life where the arts of persuasion, command, or suggestion have to be practised. The practised singer will have necessarily attended to the development and perfecting of his faculty of speech. Correct breathing is hardly more necessary for success in singing than it is for the maintenance of sound health. Attention to the varying pitch and tone cultivates the artistic faculty, and conduces to refine the manner and ennoble the emotional nature. Those who have studied singing declare that it is one of the best means of promoting physical health. For successful singing the muscles must be trained to secure that the body be well poised, that the chest be properly expanded for breathing, and that the throat be free from any kind of restraint.

The principles that regulate the choice of material for singing in school are the same as in the case of other subjects. There must be a clear understanding of the end to be attained; thereafter a carefully graduated scheme must be drawn up. Generally speaking, the simple things are best here as else-where—simple in melody, in harmony, in rhythm. As for the subjects of the songs, those dealing with the elemental emotions are naturally most suitable. Nature in her various manifestations and moods, the seasons with their characteristic notes and charms, the joys and sorrows of home and social life, noble deeds in peace and in war, these are only a few of the many subjects that never pall. In Scottish schools the works of Scotland's poets and great song-writers will naturally receive first consideration. There may be acute difference of opinion as to the advisability of teaching dialect in the primary school, but there can be no doubt whatever that it is the duty of every teacher to see that Scottish pupils leave school filled with a love for Scottish minstrelsy.

An inhabitant of one of the capitals of Buchan used to say that the rival capital was the biggest town for its size that he knew. One can safely make the claim that Scotland, considering its size and population, has the richest collection of ballads and songs on almost every conceivable subject of any country, and these have in a large proportion of cases been set to the most charming, haunting music. I would also put in a plea for giving attention to local songs in connection with the study of history and the inculcation of patriotism. Not every district can vie with the Highlands, and especially with Ayr, in the number of popular songs, but even " Gadie Rins " and " Mormond Braes " are by no means to be despised, and when the ballads and poems and songs collected by the late Gavin Greig and his assistants are published with appropriate music, the field of choice will be greatly extended for those who appreciate the song-material of the north-eastern part of Scotland.

Reference has been made to the danger that arises from the separation of one subject of school study from others. In my opinion, there should be the most intimate connection between the teaching of singing and of literature. The singing of a song in school should always be preceded by a literature lesson in miniature, to give the setting of the words, the circumstances in which they were written, the significance of the title, the stuff of the song whether subjective or objective, the appropriateness of the language to express the conception, the beauty of the melody, the character of the rhythm, and so on. Only when the pupils have entered into the spirit of the words will they sing the song with zest, enjoyment and real sympathy. If it be true, as it is, that the best literature can be appreciated only when it is read aloud, it is much more true that the best lyrics of the greatest masters of the art can have full justice done to their merits only by being studied, read aloud, and thereafter musically interpreted and expressed. I should be the very last to underestimate the importance of reasonable adherence to the school time-table—that is a matter of honour and of necessity—but I have no hesitation in saying that the poetry lesson should deal very largely with the things that can be sung. If they were actually sung after being learned by the whole class or by sections of the class, or as trios or duets or solos, they would be far more appreciated, because they would be interpreted in the spirit in which they were written, and consequently much more likely to remain permanent possessions. Teachers cannot be too grateful for the freedom which enables them thus to make the poetry lesson a delight instead of a torture, as it was in the days when a certain definite number of lines, and no more, had to be learned in the course of a year for repetition at the annual display before H.M. Inspector. Young pupils should sing and draw and play nearly half the school day. Experience proves that they learn more in this way, at least of what is worth learning, than if their " work " has no lightening.

Every normal child has a latent sense for beauty, which can be developed by suitable outlets and stimuli. Beautiful music, with its structure rhythm, melody and harmony, is specially calculated to promote this æsthetic sense. The child must indeed be poorly dowered who is not affected by the refining influences of good music. If " manners maketh man," art refines the manners, and drawing and singing are arts both readily available and potent. " Musical training is a more potent instrument than any other, because rhythm and melody find their way into secret places of the soul on which they mightily fasten, imparting grace, and making the soul graceful of him who is ill-educated." If Plato's understanding of music was wider than the modern connotation of the term, those who know will readily admit that his greater includes our less.

If there is one subject more in a state of flux than others, it is surely physical training. A generation ago pupils were allowed and expected to find their own means of sport and play, and if the matter were proposed as subject for debate a reasonable case could be made for leaving a boy to find out what was best for him in this connection. In any case, singing accompanied many of the games in the playground. Later were introduced Indian clubs and bar-bells, and the students sang during their exercises. Since that time the new methods and various modifications of them have been almost innumerable, and quite recently we seem to have almost completed the circle and to be returning to a large extent to the much more reasonable and natural system of games and racing and skipping in lieu of the more formal training. Many of these exercises may be and are accompanied by singing.

It is not at all improbable that the Jacques-Dalcroze system of eurhythmics may soon be thought worthy of a " turn " on the gymnastic stage. As his main principle seems to be that all education in music should be based on tone and rhythm, and as the essence of the method is the co-ordination of movement and music, there seems to be good ground for giving the system a trial. Confirmation of the view that there is a very intimate connection between open-air exercises and music and of their mutual beneficial influence was afforded by Captain Hulbert's book on eurythmics. During the war young men of no particular musical bent developed voices of a beauty which even a complete ignorance of how to use them could not entirely conceal. " The explanation of the sudden outburst of vocal beauty was that abundant fresh air, gymnastics, and drill had put these men in superb physical condition, and that with the improvement in their general health their voices had improved in a corresponding degree." Vocal fitness, according to Captain Hulbert, is a matter of physical fitness, and the singer is, in a sense, an athlete trained to his or her particular work.

There seems no substantial reason why girls should not sing, or be sung to, while they sew their seams, and boys while they are busy at various kinds of " practical " work. Experience proves that such an accompaniment is quite as improving, and probably not so dangerous, as the traditional concomitant of the sewing meeting for adults. When the interest has flagged and energy is for the time exhausted, three minutes at drill or singing works a wonderful change. The drooping spirits of the man are revived when the band begins to play. It is not necessary that the band or the singers be specially engaged. When the class itself, or individuals in it, provide the relief, its effect upon mind and body is specially marked. When the motion is " That primary school education should be mainly vocational," I invariably vote in the " no " lobby, but I should have some hesitation if the question referred only to singing. If it is taught on common-sense lines and in close co-ordination with other subjects, it is both immediately educative and permanently advantageous.

THE LIGHTER SIDE OF SCHOOL LIFE.

A LARGE proportion of the school day should admittedly be devoted to the basic subjects, English, calculation and writing. The demand is sometimes made that these subjects, and these only, should be taught in ordinary schools, that it is unfair that the ratepayers should bear the burden of educating other people's children in what are called ornamental subjects, such as drawing, music, cookery. It is to be feared that these critics have been born out of their time. Their protests might have been heeded fifty years ago, but for better or for worse we are all Socialists nowadays in education, except the very small minority that sends its children to private schools and at the same time enjoys the pleasure of supporting the public school.

Would pupils learn more of the three basic subjects if the whole of school time were devoted to these? Experience says they would not. A little at a time with much repetition is the very foundation of success in primary school work. Variety and the keeping up of interest must be the continual care of the successful educator. Again, the conception that a child goes to school to learn only what is useful in the way of earning a living is not an admirable nor even a worthy idea. Even a slight study of child nature without going at all deeply into the problems of psychology will be sufficient to convince the sceptic that knowledge cannot be administered to the young mind in homeopathic doses. Much of our most useful knowledge is that which we learn unconsciously. The study of the things about us, animal, plant, mineral; appreciation of and the attempt to reproduce, so as better to appreciate, beauty on earth, on sea, and in sky; care and respect for the body and its development so as to secure graceful movement, the training of our hands and of our powers of touch and sight to distinguish things that differ, these may not be strictly part of the three R's, but will anyone who has been educated within the last twenty years, or who has made it his aim actually to know what is done in schools, say that they hinder progress in real education. If such a person exists, let him consult has ingenuous nephew. Brought up on the supposedly more solid diet of the old parochial school and nurtured on the Classics, I heartily support the more modern, more educative, and much more reasonable conception of instruction now general in the best schools.

After woodwork, drawing is the school subject for which the "practical" man reserves his greatest scorn. You can never, he says, make all children artists. This critic reminds me of a teacher who advocated the dropping of this subject from the school curriculum because he could never draw himself. He should know that no attempt is made to make all pupils artists any more than to make them all authors or mathematicians or copper-plate writers. The conception underlying the giving of instruction in each of these basic subjects is that the normal child has certain faculties that are worth developing for their own sake, and for the advantage of society of which he is a member and to which he will, if duly trained, contribute something of value. The case for instruction in drawing is precisely similar. Every average child has a latent sense for beauty. Without awakening, development and guidance, this power may remain dormant, but receiving due attention it can become, and has in count-less instances already become a new eye to look out upon nature and on life.

Every healthy child likes to "make" things—in mud, in wood, with pencil, with ink. Foolish parents and teachers forbid the indulgence of this craving. They ought to rejoice in it, and gratify it as much as possible. A box of coloured crayons and some brown paper are cheap and powerful means of *real* education. Ninety-nine per cent. of children can learn to draw, as quite that percentage can be taught to sing if they are caught young enough. (I do not forget the indi-vidual who is the exception and who, having the voice of a raven, fancies that there are probably many others in similar case, especially if he has to help to pay their fees.)

Drawing should begin on the first day of a pupil's educa-tion, and the subject should receive the same expert and systematic attention as is given to what are called more important subjects. The subject needs strenuous attention. Twenty years ago we were told by superior critics who knew, in spite of their official position, almost nothing about elementary teaching, and even less about the normal child, that the only direction to be given to pupils about to draw was " Draw what you see." I have seen the plan tried, and its absurdity was soon evident. " The eye sees what it brings with it the power of seeing," and while it is true that each man has his own point of view, the sense of sight needs educating, and the eyes of different individuals, duly trained, see very much the same. In drawing there must be a system, just as in teaching to read or to count or to sing. The best teachers encourage their pupils from the start to work in various media, crayons, pencil, brush, &c. The drawing lesson is one of the most relished and educative hours of the week. From the fact that every object has an individual setting, background and foreground, the pupil comes to appreciate the importance in the relationships of life and business of harmony as opposed to discord, of the light standing out against the darker background. To put things in the best light in life need not be despicable, and the setting of objects so that the light falls upon them to good advantage is an excellent means of developing the æsthetic side of the pupil's nature.

The effort to indicate the constitution and texture of various articles, wood, earthenware, glass, &c., each requiring different treatment for its successful representation, trains the pupil to careful thought and manipulation. The relation of the different parts of a model to each other, and of the different constituents of the whole group to one another, emphasises the necessity and the advantage of developing the sense of proportion and of understanding perspective. The fact that one medium, say pencil, is more suitable than another, say charcoal, for bringing out the particular characteristics of a certain article, impresses the fact that what is good for one man may not suit his neighbour. The delineation of an object or group in black-and-white to-day, and of the same group in water-colour to-morrow, will indicate that in this connection and in the wider life of the world tastes or circumstances may differ and yet each be worthy of approval.

Allowing the pupil to bring his own specimens, to draw them in suitable settings and with appropriate materials, with due guidance from the teacher, gives him increasing confidence in his own judgment, develops initiative, and strengthens his desire to have his surroundings in life harmonious. Pupils delight in having the suggestions and criticism of their teachers and fellows in their efforts to illustrate some scene from nature, some incident of which they have read, some imaginative experience. The girl who has learned to sketch will have received some real inspiration, some uplift which will, in even moderately favourable circumstances, go with her through life. She will not be contented with drab surroundings. The etching on the wall, the touch of colour on the table, are in her case the simple but eloquent revealers of the presence of a sense of beauty. If a millionaire is in search of a method of spending money that will be permanently beneficial, let him adorn the walls of the school with really good pictures. An impression made in the years before fourteen will persist right through life. The school should be the airiest, most cheerful, most artistic house in the parish. Brought up in such surroundings, the mothers of the future will do what they can to see to it that the homes of the country are not hovels.

If you are a sceptic about the influence and utility of drawing, ask a bright pupil of fifteen to show you his portfolio. If it be true that we have travelled away from happiness because we have abandoned our simplicity and childlike delight in " meadow, grove and stream, the earth and every common thing," we had better get back on to the road whence we have strayed. If we cannot do so in person, it will be well for us to give the young a chance of searching for and finding the beautiful, which is also the true, in nature and in art. Extraordinary progress has been made in drawing methods in school during the last twenty years, but I am inclined to prophesy that even more rapid development will mark the immediate future. Be that as it may, there can be no doubt in the minds of those who have actual experience in school that the small amount of time—two hours at most—per week devoted to Art is well and profitably spent.

CONTINUATION EDUCATION FOR THE EARLY TEENS.

THE facilities provided for the primary school course have come to be regarded as fairly adequate, except that in town schools the classes are too large to permit of the teachers giving any really effective attention to individual pupils, while in the smaller rural schools the fact that a teacher has single-handed to conduct classes at six or seven different stages of advancement, or two teachers to handle three or four separate classes each, has made it impossible to give the pupils the chance that is afforded to their more fortunate fellows in centres where the teacher has to manage only one class of moderate size. For higher education the gradual extension of the number of centres has improved the facilities, but the evil effects of excessive centralisation on the health, morals and intellectual progress of distance pupils have not yet been sufficiently counteracted.

The outstanding defect of the present arrangement is the failure to supply a satisfactory course for the pupil who, owing to antecedent circumstances or the narrow outlook of his parents, or the unsuitability of the existing provision of classes, leaves school before he has received all the education from which he might have profited. In many cases he realises too late what he has lost, and I wish to suggest a combined post-qualifying day-school and evening-class course that would be of benefit to those who are free from compulsion to attend school. That many pupils at present leave school with their education in such a state that they soon forget a large part of what they have learned is by no means creditable to the country or the system, and it must be a source of danger to the welfare and the stability of the commonwealth in the future that so many of those who now possess political power as voters should be less qualified than they ought to be for the intelligent discharge of their duties as citizens. Though we shall have apparently to depend on voluntary effort on the part of pupils and others responsible for some time, I believe that a considerable degree of success is meantime possible until Education Authorities have imposed upon them the duty and responsibility of attending to the education of all adolescents who are not being otherwise educated beyond the age of fourteen. My belief in the possibility and even probability of the considerable success of such voluntary courses is confirmed by the fact that classes of this kind have been proved to be of great value where they have been organised and managed on reasonable lines. The work must be planned so as to provide full courses of three or four years' duration after the compulsory stage—*i.e.*, up to the age of fourteen. These courses must have a definite objective, and the diligence and progress of the pupil must be attested by a certificate of recognised value. Needless to say, the success of the classes depends largely on the mental attitude and outlook of the pupils, and in more than one thoroughly organised course the success of the work has been indubitable.

There are, however, grave defects in the present system so far as the average evening school is concerned. Those most in need do not, as a rule, attend. Pupils receive exemption from the day-school on condition that they attend a Continuation Class. In an overwhelming proportion of cases they never even enrol, and no penalty follows, for obvious reasons. Those who have for some cause, often preventable, been backward at school, do not join evening classes. They are in some cases too much ashamed of their ignorance; in still others they are uninterested in anything that does not contribute to the supposed enjoyment of the moment, and desire to be free from all restraint. In many of the smaller evening schools the vocational element is too prominent, and pupils take only such subjects as are likely to contribute to their material success. Such study is from every point of view preferable to none at all, but it is very desirable that the cultural side of education should receive a fair share of attention, at least in the earlier years of a continuation course. The time available is also too short. It must apparently all come off the hours of leisure, though in several of the larger centres employers find it both convenient and profitable to allow their more apt apprentices to attend classes during the day. Even of the leisure time there is available for instruction only what is left over from more attractive allurements, and it needs a strong purposeful mind to prefer the hard and only remotely beneficial to the immediately pleasureable and easy.

In order to secure that the course shall be a really educative one it must be begun early, be of reasonable duration, be homogeneous from beginning to end, and have a definite objective. I have in view, therefore, a combined day and subsequent evening course, such as is apparently being planned in several of the larger centres. One great advantage of such combination is that, if the pupil's appetite for knowledge has been whetted by a comprehensive and attractive bill of fare in the last two years of his compulsory school life, he will have all the more relish to return to finish the other courses of the meal. Moreover, there is considerable ground for the hope and belief that a fair proportion of pupils would voluntarily remain at the day school for another year, especially in times when it is difficult to get regular employment, if the course were really educative and practical.

The practical value of any course of Continuation education depends naturally on several factors, for example, its length, the number and extent of the subjects, and the nature of the certificate attainable at the conclusion. The Supplementary Course suffers greatly because of deficiencies in these respects. Too large a proportion of pupils are promoted from the primary department only when they reach the age of thirteen or over. That means that they have only just begun the study of higher and more practical subjects when they are entitled by age to leave school. If the pupil is going to study languages, a start at the age of eleven is of incalculable value. This is recognised so strongly in some schools that the study of a language is encouraged a year before the pupils leave the primary department. But in ordinary circumstances this plan is not feasible unless the " feeder " schools have an understanding with the centre that all pupils shall be studying the same language and at nearly the same speed. I am sometimes asked if it would be advisable to have special classes for backward pupils who cannot, if they are taught with normal children, hope to reach the usual standard about

the age of twelve. This is certainly very advisable, but such
a proposal would entail considerable expenditure.

In large schools there ought to be some arrangement to
secure more attention to these pupils; in smaller schools they
should get as much consideration as circumstances permit,
and in all schools they should, on reaching a certain age, get
a very large share of any practical work that is available—
cookery for both sexes, gardening, woodwork, practical
science, and so on. The old fetish of the Qualifying examination for such pupils should be finally discarded.

Suppose that suitable courses can be devised of a more
practical nature than the present literary course, and that each
of these is to last for three years. Who is to decide which
of two courses a pupil is to follow? Those who advocate an
external control examination think they score here. The
pupil who gains a high percentage of marks in the examination will take the normal literary course; his fellow who does
less well must take a course which is, or has at least up to the
present time been, less fashionable. Note the underlying
assumption. The former course is more expensive, because
the teaching is supposed to be of a more intellectual kind;
the practical course can be carried on for a smaller outlay.
That is the result of a bad tradition, and is a notion that should
be finally given up. Well-planned, well-balanced Continuation
Courses of a practical kind are just as educative for clever
pupils of a certain turn of mind as so-called literary courses,
and they cannot be run more cheaply. Suppose, however,
that the parent of the pupil who passes high refuses to allow
his son to enter for the literary course, and—a very much
harder problem because of various social and economic
factors—the father of the child who has done badly in the
external test insists that his offspring shall get the advantage
of what is called real higher education. No conceivable
arrangement of a mechanical kind will ever settle these most
insistent and everyday difficulties. Wise parents will at least
take counsel with those who have had their children under
instruction and guardianship for all the previous years of their
school life. No reliance can be placed on the result of a few
hours' special effort as compared with the experience and
testing of years.

The well-to-do parent can always get his own way. He

can send his son to an institution where he will, or at least hopes to, get for his boy the education for which he is willing to pay. On the other hand, a fair number of clever boys and girls do not receive the education to which their abilities entitle them. If they got a chance, the improved service they would afterwards give would be ample return for the capital outlay. Whether on the lines indicated or otherwise, something must be done to try to secure that a much greater proportion of pupils than at present shall have their primary school education supplemented by two years' instruction of a slightly vocational nature before they leave the day school. While I am in favour of more freedom in arranging curricula to meet varying aptitudes and objectives of pupils, I disagree with the Department when it advocates an entirely separate organisation even in subjects which are common to the Secondary and non-Secondary Group. Such a policy, except perhaps in very large centres, is calculated to undo much of the progress already made, and to evoke or perpetuate in the public mind the erroneous idea that the kind of education which is fitted to produce a learned man is unsuited for those who are to enter some department of business activity.

For the purpose of maintaining and, if possible, of extending the system of voluntary Continuation Classes until such time as the compulsory clauses of the Act of 1918 relating to the education of adolescents are brought into force, it is very desirable and important that the sympathy and active co-operation should be enlisted of all who have any influence with young people. Reference has been made to the necessity that is bound to be felt soon of having some kind of Board, national or provincial, that will be responsible for the general organisation and supervision of all forms of education. Only in this way shall we be able to get value for our money and to keep our educational system in harmony with and in a position to satisfy adequately the needs of business and professional life.

I do not advocate the establishment of mere Boards or Authorities by legal enactment. There are enough, probably more than enough, of Boards already. The success of any educational system does not depend primarily upon what may be called the administrative side. The most that external administration can accomplish is to create conditions that

are as favourable as possible to the carrying on of the daily
work of the school or college. I refer to such conditions as
suitable buildings erected as far as possible in such a way as
to satisfy modern conceptions of lighting, heating, sanitation
and so on. It is the duty of the administrators also to see
that the education and instruction are in the hands of
thoroughly educated and properly trained teachers working
under such conditions as shall tend to make them contented,
efficient and proud of their work and its influence. The
ultimate success of educational effort depends invariably on
the quality of the teaching staff. If either of these fail a
satisfactory result is impossible.

What is needed, then, to enable us to meet the needs of
the transition period, during which we must depend on
voluntary attendance at Continuation Classes, is the rousing
of interest on the part of employers of labour, of workers
(both manual and professional), and of public-spirited men
and women generally. Experience has shown that appeals
addressed to these and other sections of the community have
not gone unanswered. Long before the war the School Board
of Edinburgh was able to boast legitimately of the success of
its Continuation Classes, and to congratulate itself and the
citizens that it had had the cordial assistance of employers,
trade associations, voluntary agencies, teachers and parents.
What can be accomplished in this way is also well illustrated
by the experience of such great firms as Rowntrees, of York,
who have nearly a score of persons engaged as full-time
teachers in connection with their works, in which they employ
over five thousand workers. Of course it may be said that
the organisation of classes in a business of such magnitude
was comparatively easy, and there is something to be said
for that statement, but the point I wish to make is that the
firm found it advisable and to its interest and profit to make
provision for the education and recreation in working hours
of its employees.

Mention may be made of an even more interesting experiment from our present point of view, because it concerns not
the employees of one firm, but a class engaged on employment
that is usually looked upon as thoroughly of a blind-alley
nature and entirely unorganised. I refer to the classes in the
city of York for message boys. These classes, four in num-

ber, each met twice a week for two hours at a time, one class having its instruction on Monday forenoon from 10 to 12 and on Thursday from 2 to 4 p.m. The Committee in charge was greatly encouraged by the hearty response of the employers. The success of voluntary Continuation Classes in many centres in Scotland is due to a considerable extent to the enlightened and continuous interest taken in these classes by intelligent and disinterested leaders in the various towns. In this connection mention may be made of what has been achieved in Peterhead, where there has been in operation for many years a system of Evening School work of which the success has been uninterrupted and ever-increasing. The burgh has been fortunate in its administrators, and even more so in the organiser of its courses and classes. The prospectus and arrangements are models for those who wish to develop Continuation education on sound and modern lines.

Doubtless it is the success of these and similar voluntary agencies that led to the incorporation in the Education Act of 1918 of Section 25, to the following effect:—" It shall be the duty of every Education Authority within three months after the first election thereof to establish an Advisory Council consisting of persons qualified to represent the views of bodies interested in education, for the purpose of advising the Authority on matters of educational interest relating to the education area, and the Authority shall take into consideration any advice or representation submitted to them by the local Advisory Council."

That section has always seemed to me wise, reasonable and necessary. We are continually reminded that our educational system is not sufficiently in touch with the actual needs and concerns of the business and other life of the community. Here is provision expressly made for the focusing and expression of the views of people who are necessarily in touch with live issues. The section of the Act is not permissive but compulsory, but so far as I can find out by frequent inquiry the Advisory Council has, in certain areas at least, been appointed, but has done no effective work of any kind. Objections have been raised to the expense which would be entailed by the meetings of these Councils, but I refuse to believe that the members selected to serve on these Councils would not be willing to defray from their

5

own resources the small outlay that would be required to
enable the Councils to function. Some people have a shrewd
suspicion that bureaucracy does not wish outsiders to have
any say in educational administration. It is high time that
advantage be taken of the services of those who, being in
touch with and cognisant of the needs of the actual affairs
of life, are in an excellent position to advise as to the most
suitable kinds of Continuation education.

The advice and suggestions of these Advisory Councils
need to be suppplemented and reinforced by the experience
and co-operation of existing organisations and associations
whose primary aim is not so much educational as social or
recreative or even quasi-political. Much may be expected
from the efforts and experience of the Workers' Educational
Association and similar bodies, and provision was made in
the 1918 Act for securing such help. The section dealing
with this point has not yet been brought into force, but it
is to be hoped that in the larger centres at least it may be
used in the spirit if not in the letter. It provides for communi-
cating and co-operating with " associations or committees
of employers and workmen concerned in the registration or
supervision of apprentices in trades where apprentices are
employed, or with similar associations or committees in trades
or businesses where young persons, though not apprenticed
thereto, have the prospect of regular employment therein in
later years."

It should also be immediately possible, in the words of
the Act, to " register and classify young persons according
to their employment, and to have regard to the educational
requirements of such young persons with respect alike to
their present and their prospective employments." Every
Education Authority has in its possession the data that are
required to secure such registration and classification, for it
is now several years since the inauguration of the new regime,
and the names, ages and educational attainments of all young
persons between fourteen and seventeen years of age are
immediately available.

The question of the further education of the adolescent
is closely connected with that of the apprentice system.
According to the principle and practice of the old Guild system
the master was responsible not only for teaching the learner

all the details of his craft, but also for securing that due attention was given to the training of the intelligence and character of his apprentices. Even in fairly recent times, in country districts at least, apprentices lived under the same roof as their masters, were treated as members of the family so far as board was concerned, and were subject to the same rules of order and discipline. In these days the master had to make out of the apprentice a " man " in both the narrower and more generous sense of the word. Modern conditions have almost entirely broken down the apprentice system as formerly understood, but employers are still to be found who have an interest in the intellectual and social development of their younger workers.

Much valuable work could undoubtedly be accomplished in the planning and carrying out of voluntary Continuation Classes by the co-operation of representatives of various bodies such as the Universities, Education Authorities, Chambers of Commerce, Rotary Clubs, Workers' Educational Associations, Boy Scouts, Girl Guides' organisations, and of parents and teachers. The work is urgent for both educational and social reasons. Our neighbours and competitors are devoting great energy to Continuation Classes. We cannot afford to lag behind.

Reference has already been made to the advisability and even necessity of keeping the system of Continuation Classes in close touch with the industrial and business life of the community. It is sometimes made a ground for complaint against the school that it is out of harmony with the aims and needs of a practical age. If this criticism is justified to any extent, the fault cannot be ascribed entirely to those responsible for the school courses and their carrying out. But that reproach is being gradually removed by the establishment of non-language courses. Business men should make their opinions and requirements known. If these are founded on sound premises and built on experience they will receive the respect and attention which it is possible to give them, always provided that it be remembered that school education must never be mainly vocational. I admit that the main post-Qualifying course is too literary and much too restricted in its range. The influence of the teaching profession, backed by the demands of organised business men, is certain sooner rather than later to introduce an intermediate course of a more practical kind for those who are preparing for a non-professional career. While, however, such a modification is both reasonable and practicable, it is only after the pupil has, at the age of fifteen or thereby, finished a three years' higher course in which central subjects predominate that he can begin on strictly vocational lines with any assurance that the progress will be solid.

The chief desideratum at this time of transition is, in my opinion, to arouse and maintain the interest not only of the pupil, but of the responsible part of the community. There will have to be a renewed effort to pull all together if the wheels of the national life and industry are again to turn easily and quickly. The interests of society and of the individual are never really antagonistic except in the distorted imagination of the revolutionary or " diehard." When the master and the man come together to confer with the professional educator and the disinterested enthusiast for education, it will be found that the education which best discovers and develops the latent powers of the individual is at the same time that which renders the best service to the general progress of the community.

A very important point requires consideration at this stage. The clauses of the 1918 Act which make attendance at school compulsory up to the age of fifteen are not yet in operation. What steps can be taken at present, what inducements can be offered to encourage pupils to attend school until they have completed a course practically equal to the existing three years' course in extent at least if not in content? Attendance for this purpose may be made in either of two ways. Beginning at the age of twelve, a pupil would have completed his course of three years about one year after the date when the law at present allows him to cease attendance. When unemployment is rife it would seem reasonable that parents should encourage their children to continue to attend school until they have a definite promise of regular work. It must be admitted, of course, that this is nearly a counsel of perfection if the breadwinner is himself out of employment. There are, however, many cases where this extra year of attendance might easily be afforded if parents and pupils could be wooed by attractive courses of immediate and prospective value. Many pupils must, on the other hand, for the present at least, have their studies interrupted when they reach the age of fourteen, and it should be perfectly practicable to arrange evening classes where the work would follow without interruption that of the day school.

I calculate that three sessions of intensive study at such evening courses would be practically the equivalent of the third year of the day school course. I am well aware of the substantial objections that can be made to dependence on evening school classes as a substitute for full-time courses, but in view of existing financial stringency I am sure that the idea is capable of realisation, and if such courses are offered there will be no lack of enrolments. Every encouragement should be given to pupils to complete the three years' course at the day school. But where for satisfactory reasons a pupil is able to take only two years before he must leave the day school, he should find it not only possible, but comparatively easy, to complete his course by evening school work, and thus become entitled to a certificate of about the same value as that obtained by his more fortunate mate whose school attendance has not been interrupted.

As in many other departments of activity very much, nearly everything, depends on a timely beginning. Pupils must begin at or before the age of twelve. If they " qualify " later they lose interest in education, and no amount of prompting or encouragement will rekindle the vanished enthusiasm. Much heat and energy have been spent on the discussion of the question of the qualifying test, which, after all, is the simplest thing imaginable. It can be managed satisfactorily to the pupil's interest, and consequently for the good of the country, only by those who know the child's disposition and ability, his bent and outlook as a result of years of personal contact, and who take counsel with those who have learned their business in the school of experience. Not the qualifying examination needs considering, but what is to be done for pupils who are, in the opinion of the responsible teachers, ready to profit by higher courses planned to be of really practical value.

Now is the time for consultation between business men and educationists to plan such courses. Chambers of Commerce and similar bodies should be asked to say what they find defective in modern education. (When they criticise they should remember that a boy of fourteen cannot be expected to have the education of a grown man.) They would at the same time indicate how far they think it advisable that education should have a vocational bias. What the majority of business men probably desire is that their apprentices should have been educated on broad general lines suited to develop intelligence, accuracy and some degree of initiative, and that the teacher should not try to teach what may have to be unlearned in the actual work of the office or the warehouse.

There are certain outside examinations which aspirants for work are called upon to face. It should surely be possible, as from every point of view it is desirable, that there should be a co-ordination of such examinations as that set for banking work with ordinary school and continuation examinations. Business men should agree to accept certificates granted on the satisfactory conclusion of a course as to whose details they have been consulted, and it would be only reasonable that they should give a distinct preference for engagement and promotion to the holders of such passports. The intellectual benefit to the pupil is not always a sufficient inducement to study for young people of a certain age. It may, however, be warrantably reinforced by an appeal to the more materialistic and profitable side, and this again may justly be supplemented by the laying of much greater stress than in the past on the social and recreative side.

RURAL SCHOOLS.

IT is probably no exaggeration to say that of the many educational problems that are pressing for solution that of a suitable education for those who spring from the soil, and are intended to make their living by its cultivation, is the most urgent. No one who loves the country, no one who cares for the welfare of the commonwealth, can see without sorrow the growing tendency of the younger generation to leave the country districts and flock to the towns.

Agriculture is still the greatest individual industry in this country. Now and then Governments seem to realise afresh its importance, and efforts are made to provide means of removing or relieving the disabilities under which the industry labours, but the efforts are generally spasmodic, and in the meantime country depopulation proceeds apace. The causes of this are, of course, by no means simple. Some have their origin in what might superficially be called restlessness, the desire for more brightness in life and the hope and belief that existence in a more populous centre will be less monotonous. Many of those who are more ambitious are willing to face the comparative hardships and privations that await the emigrant to Canada, convinced as they are that it is more easy to make good in a land where convention and tradition are less powerful, where opportunity is wider for themselves and the children they hope to rear. These and other causes are gradually draining rural Scotland of many whom from almost every point of view it is desirable to retain on the soil; but there can be no doubt at all that the question of securing a suitable education for their families weighs largely with many of those who migrate.

The assertion is sometimes made that there is now assured " the national birthright of every Scottish boy and girl of good ability—namely, an indefeasible claim of access to the highest educational opportunities which the country has to give." The boast is by no means true even so far as a University education is concerned; with regard to a scientific education suitable for rural parishes, there can be no question that we have done little more than envisage the problem.

A Church Committee asserted some time ago that the average school teacher knows little about nature or agricultural pursuits, and that a new type of specially trained teacher is needed, particularly for the one-teacher school. One would like to know on what evidence the committee came to this conclusion about the average school teacher in country districts. It is no exaggeration to say that over 80 per cent. of the country schoolmasters were born in the country and are in close touch and sympathy with the main industry. Many of them are gardeners of no mean ability, and their school gardens are centres of considerable interest and profit to the pupils. While, however, it is very desirable, one would even say necessary for his own contentment and happiness, that the country teacher should have a keen interest in the scenes and work of the country, there are from the educational point of view requirements not less important. The first essential is that the teacher be thoroughly educated. Agriculture is, above all things, a practical industry, and the farmer does not desire or need any one to teach him his business.

Many of the old schoolmasters who were so highly and in many cases so justly extolled (after they were dead) knew very little about agriculture, but they were for the most part men of sound scholarship and common sense. The times have changed, and we must change with them. Too little attention was then given to science and its bearing on and service to practical life. This defect must be and is to some extent being remedied; but a little superficial knowledge of quasi-science will not make up for the absence of the deeper matters of literary culture and the truly scientific and philosophic mind. What is desired in the schoolmaster is brains and aptitude for teaching. Possessing these, he will be at least tolerated and receive a modicum of respect.

The same committee expressed the opinion that the centralisation policy has been carried too far, and the travelling which it entails was strongly condemned. So far as young children are concerned, there is no doubt a good deal of justification for this statement. A considerable amount of time, energy and money is wasted under prevailing conditions. In trying to find a remedy, it is well to remember the cause of the disorder. Some twenty years ago, when the Department, interpreting the almost unanimous opinion that the time had come when the educational basis should be broadened by the compulsory introduction of science and drawing, issued its regulations for the establishment of higher grade departments to take the place of the rather nondescript upper sections of ordinary schools, most of the more progressive School Boards, with greater or less alacrity, made provision for the teaching of the new subjects. Those that were first in the field with reasonable proposals had these, of course, at once recognised by a Department which was anxious to give its new policy an auspicious start.

With very few exceptions these higher grade schools have been extraordinarily successful. The percentage of their primary pupils taking the higher grade course, and the proportion of these that stay on for the full course are considerably higher than in the larger centres, where the conditions militate against hard and continuous study. In many other parishes the School Board would not move. Rather than face an expenditure that would have entailed a temporary paltry increase on the rates, they took up an attitude of dour and cantankerous opposition. In a few of these parishes the failure to advance with the times did not mean a heavy blow to educational efficiency, because in these areas, to a considerable extent owing to a parsimonious policy, no attention had for many years been paid to higher instruction. But in not a few parishes where there was a real educational tradition, where first-rate students were prepared every year for the training colleges, and whose schools thus performed most necessary work in helping to provide well-educated and capable teachers, no argument or even cajoling on the part of Department or other mentors was of any avail. The chance was lost. Repentance came too late when neighbouring parishes had provided accommodation and equipment in excess of their own requirements. So from these dilatory parishes the pupils who desire even the first stages of higher education have continued, relay after relay, to travel to the central school. When blame is being apportioned it is well to be as just as possible.

It may now be possible to establish a centre for higher education in every parish where advanced instruction was given from 1872 to the end of the century. What is necessary and practicable is the provision in at least one school in every civil parish of facilities for the literary, scentific and, to some extent, vocational education of children up to the age of fourteen or fifteen. To avoid misconception and misrepresentation, it is necessary to state that this proposal does not necessarily entail the providing of additional staff. Nor does it mean that every parish shall become a direct feeder of the University. But it is possible to provide in every parish for pupils up to the age of fourteen or fifteen an education that will combine in due proportion literary, scientific and recreative elements, and at the same time form a sufficient preparation for pupils who desire to continue their day-school education at a school giving a full secondary course, and for those who, requiring to earn their living during the day, are willing to study at continuation classes. This maintaining of the present standard postulates that there must be no reduction of the teaching staff in three or four-teacher schools unless there is a serious and probably permanent decline in the attendance. It lies with those who are interested in the material comfort and intellectual development of the young people in their parishes to insist that the existing facilities shall not be reduced and that, where possible, extended opportunities shall be available for those who desire to take advantage of them.

The question of the actual extent to which the parish school did prepare its pupils for the University in former days is rather difficult to settle definitely. The idea underlying the system of having in every parish a school capable of carrying its pupils from the infant stage to the end of the compulsory standard is a very attractive one. In such a school there are no violent transitions. No time is lost through the pupils having to suffer from any change of gauge in the course of the journey.

If the methods followed are logical and modern, time is not wasted in learning what experience may prove to be non-essential or even unnecessary. The pupil can be promoted from class to class whenever the responsible teachers consider promotion advisable. Much greater freedom of classification is possible. To some considerable extent, in smaller schools, classes can with advantage be combined for instruction in certain branches—for example, literature and its allied subjects, history, geography and civics. If a pupil is backward in one subject, he may be transferred to a lower class during part of the day for extra tuition in that branch. An advantage of first-rate importance, and one that is capable of realisation only in this class of school, is that pupils who are so deficient in mental aptitude that they will never pass a written examination of the type commonly known as the qualifying test, but who have some turn for work with their hands, can without any disturbance of the routine work of the school be drafted to receive practical instruction for several hours a week. Such pupils sometimes show themselves quite adept at woodwork, cookery and even experimental science of a simple kind. Moreover, the fresh interest which the new study creates has an excellent reflex influence on their arithmetical work. They seem to discover a reason for applying themselves to what was formerly a mere task. The factors that make for success in the education of pupils are very numerous, and some of them are rather incalculable, but there is no doubt the psychological element has hitherto received far too little attention, and this " self-contained " type of school affords the most favourable conditions for knowing, taking account of, and making allowance for the pupil's home circumstances, his intellectual ability, and the outlook upon life of himself and those who influence him.

Any policy which tends to lower the prestige of a school that has real educational traditions is greatly to be deprecated. Any reduction of educational facilities and opportunities which is not absolutely necessary has a baneful effect not only on the particular classes that are immediately affected, but on the whole work of the school. It is the experience of some of the older and most successful teachers that the dropping of higher instruction in their schools owing to the parsimony and narrow outlook of the former managers, immediately lowered the efficiency and tone of their schools. The incentive to excel and the desire to keep up the reputation of the parish school seemed to vanish. An education tradition needs a long time to grow; it can be destroyed very quickly. I should like to put in a very earnest plea for the preservation of the status of the parish school where it has succeeded in maintaining itself up to the present, and for its resuscitation wherever circumstances make that possible.

Proposals are sometimes made for the closing of small schools. These are of two kinds—those that are independent units, and those, called side-schools, that are to some extent under the supervision of the head teacher of a neighbouring school. To the former class belong schools with an average attendance of some ten or twenty pupils. It is hardly necessary to point out that such schools are economically expensive. The grant depends on the average attendance. The salary of the teacher is fixed according to the number of years of recorded service. Another difficulty is that it is very difficult to induce teachers to accept appointments to such schools, remote as most of them are from most of what are considered the conveniences of life and from all usual forms of entertainment and instruction. For these reasons certain Authorities find it incumbent on them to offer an additional money payment, which varies according to the locality of the school, as a sort of bait. That, of course, only aggravates the difficulty so far as the Authority's finances are concerned.

The proposal to send younger, and therefore less highly paid, teachers to these schools is hardly feasible. Inexperienced teachers need guidance, encouragement and warning during their years of provisional service. It is unsound in principle and unsatisfactory in practice to let them experiment on pupils, however few. The only young teachers who are willing to go to these inaccessible regions are those who have a passionate love for the solitary life in the wide and windy spaces, or who, as it is euphemistically put, are resolved to fulfil their natural destiny. The easiest solution of the problem is to close the school. The proposal is easy; to carry it out is invidious and may lead to unpopularity, which cannot always be risked. The school was not built without reason. It was needed when it was erected. In the opinion of those whose interests it serves it is needed still. The rate-payers in the district contribute their legal quota to the expense of education, and demand that they shall have at least the minimum facilities that the law allows. If it is proposed to staff the school with unqualified teachers, the parents naturally and properly protest and refuse to have their children experimented upon and probably neglected. Tentative efforts at the elimination of what those living in more populous districts consider necessary facilities have proved abortive, and it may be taken for granted that no popularly-elected body will be allowed to go far in this direction unless satisfactory means can be discovered of bringing the pupils affected to a neighbouring school where the buildings and staff are already in existence and reasonably sufficient.

The question that demands an answer, therefore, is— can means be found of conveying the pupils in these small schools to one or other of the larger schools in the district? One would like to say the vicinity instead of the district, but most of the small schools have no near neighbours. A solution of the problem which naturally suggests itself, and which as a matter of fact has already been tested, is to find board and lodgings for those children near to a central school; but the difficulties in the way of carrying this out are both numerous and formidable. For a really good home no satisfactory substitute has ever been found, or ever can be. What to outsiders may seem by no means desirable as a home may be quite attractive to those who have found in it all the love and attention that they have ever known. For the physical comfort and welfare of pupils attending secondary schools, training centres and similar institutions, the establishment of hostels is very desirable for one reason, among several others, that many of these students have reached an age when it is essential that they should be trained not only how to learn, but also how to join their fellows in the social and recreative activities of life.

The children in these outlying districts, however, are all of tender years. To separate them from parental influence and all the associations and attachments of their own homes, even for five days out of seven, is unwise. If they go home for the week-end the expense of transport has to be faced, and the means of conveyance are usually non-existent. Most of the parents, belonging to the class of shepherds, ghillies or farm servants, have no pony or trap of their own, and are often not in a position to contribute to the expense of transport even if a regular means be available. If residence near the centre is continuous except during holiday periods, the strain of absence from home, with all its attendant drawbacks and inconveniences, is immensely increased. Even if in the majority of instances the parents' consent were secured— which is a very generous supposition—there still remains the insuperable physical difficulty—there are, as a rule, no houses in which the children could be lodged. Well-disposed people are willing for a time to oblige by giving up part of their own scanty accommodation, but water is not so thick as blood, and interest not based on natural affection is apt to wane.

Towards the end of the war, and for some time after the armistice, we were assured that most of the difficulties experienced in remote and trackless areas in the transport of goods, passengers, mails, &c., would be overcome by utilising the aeroplane and the airship. Every morning one or other of these was to pick up bairns from the hillside crofts and the wayside clachan, and convey them swiftly and in comfort to a suitable centre of instruction, taking them home again in the afternoon. Pupils who, on cycle or on foot, had been experiencing all the rigours of the northern climate in their daily journeys to and from higher grade schools were led to picture, for themselves probably and for their successors certainly, conditions of locomotion almost luxurious. But the vision has fled with many others conceived in those halcyon days, and will not return soon, so far at least as concerns this phase of school life.

Descending from the air, we seem really to reach firm ground when our thoughts centre on the land motor car, van, lorry, or char-a-banc. So far as the problem of transport in districts with good or even fairly good roads is concerned, motor-power may safely be said to have provided a solution, at least where the amount of traffic offering is sufficient to make a motor service remunerative. In favourable circumstances the experimental stage has been reached and successfully passed, and our American cousins have shown us the way in using the motor for the conveyance of pupils to school.

Proposals for closing all the departments of even a small school are sure to meet with strenuous opposition in almost every individual instance unless the particular area affected is unfortunate enough to have on the Education Authority no resident representative or one whose interests are not primarily educational. There is, however, a line of less resistance, and it is one that is sure to have more advocates. Superficially it is less drastic and more reasonable; educationally its consequences are calculated to be disastrous unless extreme precautions are taken to safeguard the legitimate interests of the pupil, which are paramount.

Suppose there are in one parish two schools, each with two teachers, and having between them a total roll of one hundred pupils. If the teachers have approximately the same number of scholars in attendance, two teachers will find quite enough to do with six or seven classes, especially if due attention is given to the instruction of the older pupils in practical subjects. If distance permitted, one of these schools could be closed and the work could be consolidated in the other, where all the hundred pupils could be efficiently taught by three teachers. Thus the salary of one teacher would be saved. But law and common-sense agree in declaring that pupils of school age must not have to walk more than three miles to school, so neither school can be entirely dispensed with. Considerable support is being found for a middle course, that of keeping the infant and junior divisions of both schools in existence and full activity, but compelling all pupils over ten years of age to attend one of the schools. If the number of these older pupils is large enough to reduce sufficiently the attendance at one school, all the work of the smaller school will be thrown on one teacher, and two will still be sufficient for the larger. There seems to be considerable diversity of opinion as to the number of pupils that one teacher can handle. Some say forty, others thirty, and some, remembering the halcyon days when the parish schoolmaster taught all classes from infants to University entrants, are not particular to state a definite number. These problems are easy of solution so long as one does not enter the school.

Difficulty would probably be experienced in inducing or even compelling certain of the pupils over ten years of age to face the extended journey fixed for the older pupils, but the problem should be easier now that all the schools in a county are under one Authority which is not restricted or fettered as School Boards were by questions of local rating and petty jealousies. If one school is too far from the home of the pupil there is probably more convenient for him a school in a neighbouring parish where he can find the necessary facilities.

The question of Government grant must also be considered. Authorities receive £130 in respect of each teacher employed, and £75 in respect of each teacher employed in day schools under the management of the Authority in excess of the number required to provide one teacher for every thirty-six scholars receiving instruction in such schools. This is a fairly generous inducement to rural Authorities to be as liberal as possible in their staffing arrangements, and a reasonable and agreed-on system of transference and promotion would tend to keep the financial burden of additional staff within bearable limits, and at the same time encourage teachers by giving recognition to those who had done good service in a smaller sphere. I do not advocate any policy of staffing all smaller schools with teachers who are younger and therefore less expensive, but, generally speaking, it is quite possible to arrange that experience and higher remuneration go to the more responsible post.

Whether it will be advisable to close a school or any department of it will therefore depend on circumstances to be considered on each individual case. The local contribution that would require to be made to enable the extra grant of £75 to be claimed might be so small that it would be inadvisable, even foolish in many cases, to endanger educational efficiency by pursuing an over-zealous policy of centralisation. Generally speaking, where a school has been provided with reasonable equipment for carrying on primary and supplementary work and is quite efficient, its status should not be altered until what is likely to be a permanent reduction in its attendance has come about. It is easy to cripple and even to destroy a useful institution; it is difficult to set it on its legs again.

Unfortunately there are more cases than there ought to be of pupils being retained in primary schools for months and even years after they have received all the really effective education that the resources and teachers of the school can give. Many of such scholars are within reasonable distance of schools which have all the equipment, accommodation and staff required to provide (and actually supplying) full courses suited to varying needs and different capacities. But sentiment, misplaced enthusiasm, and notions even less admirable than these have hitherto been allowed to prevail. These pupils reach the age of fourteen with the intellectual outfit of children of eleven, and have acquired habits of indifference and laziness that make them the despair of any one who has been rash enough to employ them without inquiry into their antecedents. I have every sympathy with parents who realise, often too late, that their boys are not fully employed during their last year at school. This is the time when a pupil learns to work or become a trifler. If the school does not provide him with a sufficient field of literary and practical grain he should be threshing in his father's barn.

The policy of centralisation has been in full operation in England for some time. Parents and school managers, as opposed to the Education Authorities, have been protesting in such areas as Gloucestershire and Wiltshire against what they regard as the serious hardship entailed by their children having to travel much farther to school. In Rutlandshire the Authorities lend bicycles, with the option of purchase, to pupils who are compelled to travel considerable distances to school.

So far as theory is concerned, the advantages are nearly all on the side of consolidation. The larger school building is much more likely to be of a modern type, though it is only fair to say that many of the smaller schools in such a county as Inverness are most substantially and even artistically constructed. They are, indeed, models in that respect, though in many cases more attention seems to have been given to external appearance than to the reasonable requirements of accommodation and convenience. Again, the larger school and its pertinents are more likely to be kept in a decent state of repair. The sanitary arrangements, which even in the larger and more populous counties often leave so much to be desired, will be such as will support, not detract from, the instruction and efforts of the teachers to produce a healthy sentiment among the pupils, and therefore in the community, in favour of decent living. Arrangements for thorough cleaning every day of all school premises, and regular attention to the keeping of playgrounds, are comparatively easy

6

for the larger school; in a small school the teacher is literally maid of all work, educational and manual. Equipment in the way of school furnishings such as maps, charts, materials for drawing, which would at once be refused if applied for by each small school, might reasonably be afforded for the larger centre.

A blank in the educational system which educationists have always regretted could be filled. There is no class of pupil for whom less has been done, or who better deserves that justice should be done, than the rural boy or girl of twelve years of age and over, who is compelled to remain in attendance at a small school till the law allows him or her to leave. I have heard parents complain time and again of this waste of precious years, and capable and well-qualified teachers sympathising with the complaints but powerless to find a remedy, because the powers that be refused to face the small outlay that would have secured the modest equipment that had been often asked. Rural depopulation has had more causes than one, and the treatment of the small school by those who should have taken a pride in the maintenance and advancement of its status has not been the least. The early years of the twentieth century were marked educationally by a strong consciousness of the need for developing and extending the scientific and practical side of the school curriculum. Classes for the further instruction of teachers were eagerly taken advantage of, and statistics prove that teachers were zealous in securing the necessary qualification to give instruction in one or more branches, such as physics and chemistry, woodwork, gardening, cookery. Many of them, however, have never had an opportunity of teaching these subjects because of the refusal of the existing managers to supply the essential apparatus which before the war would have cost only a few sovereigns. The opportunity, not indeed of making an advance, but of conserving the educational position of these small parish schools was lost, and the present price of scientific equipment makes any policy of extension very hard to accomplish.

The reproach is often made that education takes the Highlanders away from home, and enthusiasts affirm that if due attention were paid to instruction in Gaelic young men and women would not feel so keenly and answer so readily the call of the south. Considering, however, the poverty of the soil in many districts and the want of an outlet for the energies of the members of the family, the lad who has ambition can as a rule gain more material success in the larger business and industrial centres. There is no finer material for an educator to work upon so far as literary and cultural studies are concerned. The Celt is imaginative, and his sense for fine things has been developed by centuries of contact with nature in her more majestic scenes and moods. He therefore responds readily to the appeal of the beautiful in art. But there is reason in the objection to confining education mainly to literary subjects. In spite of the serious handicaps already mentioned, considerable progress has been made in extending facilities for practical education in country districts. Luckily, there is little need for the erection of new buildings, though the same cannot be said of equipment. The key of the situation is the teacher. Effective instruction can be given only by well-qualified teachers, well-trained, interested in country life and working under conditions that are calculated to make reasonable people contented with their sphere, conscious of the greatness of their opportunity, and proud of their work. The small school must always suffer in this respect in competition with the larger. In the latter it is possible to have division of labour, seeing that there are two, three or even four teachers to share the instruction according to qualification and predilection. It needs a teacher of unusual enthusiasm and uncommon endurance to handle all the classes and all the subjects that call for attention if the small school is in any adequate degree to meet modern demands.

IS THERE A SPECIFICALLY RURAL PROBLEM IN SCOTTISH EDUCATION?

FROM one point of view the answer to the question is in the negative. The foundations of a sound education are, generally speaking, the same for all classes of what are called normal pupils. It must, however, be remembered that while the foundations are largely the same in substance from age to age, the elements are not fixed and unvarying either in number or in content or even in educational value. Just as each age must translate a great classic into the language and idiom of its own time if it is to get from that classic the full and exact meaning which it contains for the particular age, so every generation must decide what parts of the broad field of knowledge most and best deserve cultivation for and by its young people. But no scheme of education can at the present time be considered reasonably adequate that does not provide for the giving of due attention to the following departments of knowledge. At the top of the list on every ground of utility and sentiment comes instruction in the mother-tongue and all the sub-divisions that may and should be grouped with it, including Literature and Language; History—Scottish, British and Colonial, to some extent at least; Civics and Geography. A reasonable amount of time must, of course, be allotted to Calculation in its various phases and applications, and in this connection more care than in the past should be given to the reasons for the various steps of the process. Mechanical accuracy is not difficult to secure. There is something more difficult and much more valuable to be attained—training of the logical faculty which Mathematical subjects are specially well calculated to effect. The investigation at first hand and under expert guidance of the phenomena of Nature, of all that lies open to our eyes and ears, is being more and more recognised as a basic constituent in modern education. How easily do we fall into the habit of living regardless of those elemental things about us in which Wordsworth declares that one secret of happiness lies. How many of us close our eyes, if they were ever awakened, to what Carlyle calls the open secret, open to all and understood by so few. No sound scheme of education can afford to neglect the cultivation of the power of seeing and appreciating the beautiful in nature, in art and in life. Nor can we afford to despise the need for the inculcation and development of the social sense, of the art of living not as hermits, but as members of a community, bound as heirs of a great tradition to serve, not merely to use and to enjoy. One other educational feature now recognised as valuable is that of trying to teach the pupil or at least of putting him into an attitude that will enable him to learn to enjoy leisure wisely, an art that is difficult indeed, but was never more needed than in our own age.

No matter where education is carried on, whether in town or country, at home or abroad, any satisfactory scheme of primary instruction must provide for these essential subjects, as well as concurrent opportunity for the schools co-operating with the home and other ameliorative agencies in enforcing the fundamental duties of honour, service, loyalty to principle and respect for the rights of others.

There are, however, points of difference between urban and rural life, and of these account must be taken both in government and education, or the results will be disastrous. The evidences of vacillation in agricultural policy on the part of successive governments are only too patent. The effects of the industrial revolution, of the consequent migration of the rural population to the towns and to countries across the sea, and of the opening up and development of lands more favourably situated and more fertile than ours, have not yet been understood by our legislators. Meantime our country is being depleted of its most promising inhabitants, and the drift will not be stopped by any artificial barrier. Agricultural Colleges are excellent in their way and most useful as supplementary to the work of the farm and for showing the practical farmer how science is an indisputable aid to success. The policy of establishing small holdings is theoretically sound,

but the successful smallholder will not be found in the towns-
man who has spent his life in circumstances that have made
him quite incapable of adapting himself to the thrift, the
stern application and even the drudgery that are constant
concomitants of life on a croft. The hands of the clock can
never be turned back with impunity. The problem of rural
prosperity must be solved by retaining in the country districts
those who are already there and their children, and in the
promotion of this essential aim Education must play its part.

While maintaining that Primary Education must never be
directly vocational, I hold that it is both possible and advisable
to devise schemes of instruction that will appeal to the experience, the instincts and the outlook of country children. There
is only too much ground for the assertion that the Educational
policy and plans of the last fifty years have had regard principally for the needs of the town child. We need to realise
that there is a specifically rural problem in education. No
doubt the inhabitant of the country district has qualities in
common with his town brother, but his environment and
his occupation have developed in him certain definite characteristics, such as independence, doggedness, capacity for
work, as well as a strong vein of conservatism. He is in
touch with Nature and deals with her at first hand. " Up
from the soil rise the currents of life and energy. Up from
the common soil, up from the quiet heart of the people rise
joyously to-day streams of hope and determination "—
(President Wilson.) These qualities are essential to the continued prosperity of the country as a whole. They will not
persist without cultivation. They are in danger of extinction
for such typical reasons as the following. The standard of
material comfort for the country worker is poor. Wages are
low; housing accommodation is indifferent and too often
thoroughly unsatisfactory; educational facilities are not over-
abundant. The conditions of work are hard, with alternate
high temperatures and low, exposure to sun and rain with
consequent rheumatism and similar ills. There are few
chances of promotion for the breadwinner and even smaller
prospect of suitable situations for the adolescents of the
family. The country is dull so far as amusements are concerned. The stimulus of congenial company, of lectures and
other means of intellectual improvement is seriously lacking.

There is, of course, another side to the picture, but on the whole a considerable proportion of the more brainy, more ambitious young people who have to live in country districts are inclined to be restless and envious of what they consider the superior attractions of city life.

In view of this state of matters, it behoves us to consider what is the cause of the unrest, and to try to find a remedy. On the principle that it is wise to learn from the man on the spot, even though he may be prejudiced, it may be helpful to summarise briefly some of his criticisms of the school, its working and its products. The critic alleges such faults as the following. Rural education is too bookish. It is useless, foolish and wasteful to give " advanced " instruction to boys and girls who will never make any use of what they are learning. Too much education produces a distaste for rural life and for manual work generally. Education makes children despise the simple life of the country, and in some cases even their own homes and parents. Modern education makes young people unsettled, and induces them to migrate to towns as soon as possible. A boy must begin farm work not later than at twelve or thirteen years of age if he is to become proficient. The ordinary school curriculum is planned in the interest of those who are to use their heads, not their hands. Harrow may train " heads "; Hoxton must train " hands," which, being translated for our present purpose, means Education produces too many " fine " people whose ambition is to wear a black coat.

I have given these criticisms exactly as they have been stated to me time and again. To each one of them a more or less satisfactory retort could be made, but meantime I merely remark that we are living in an age when the humanitarian motive and the community sense and practice are being more and more strongly developed and applied. The general conscience of the community has decided that the child shall not be exploited in the interest of the employer or even of the unreasonable parent; young people have only one chance of being educated in the ordinary sense of that word. No doubt some of them may be willing to leave school prematurely in the hope of escaping from what at a difficult age they may consider galling restraint or of earning enough to make them " independent "; but in its own interest, and

with a view to obviating heavy future expenditure on unem-
ployables, the State is morally bound to see that every child
without exception receives the best educational equipment
that can be supplied. It is hardly necessary to point out that
a school is not and cannot possibly be a place where each
pupil shall be prepared to fill a certain niche. Who has the
ability, who is willing to take the responsibility of deciding
for the pupil and of arranging for the inevitable misfits?
What the school must aim at is to equip the pupils for living
as men and women and as citizens with duties and rights,
whatever may be the occupations to which choice or in most
cases necessity may lead them. " The mind is the principal
thing," and in the planning and carrying out of school work
we must have the training of the mind, the will and the
emotions as the principle objective.

But this view of the chief end of education is not incon-
sistent with giving considerable attention to the cultivation
of the practical side at almost every stage of the school course.

The pupil's environment can be made the starting point
and the source of material and interest for the teaching.
H. G. Wells was in his early days a schoolmaster, but he got
scared and ran away. He went out to other things where,
as he expected, the work was easier and the conditions of
employment better. He became tired of dealing with in-
tractable material, of putting up with stupid interference from
parents and Education Authorities. Yet he believed that
the teacher would be the soul and centre of a reconstructed
human life, and therefore he preached to teachers " shame-
lessness, arrogance and aggression—they should take up and
take hold of the world." Teachers may smile at their taking
hold of the world, but, after all, the world for most of us is
the little bit near to us. We shall not be held responsible for
the rest. Is it possible to apply Mr Wells' school philosophy
to the solution of the problem of rural education?

In another chapter I have dealt with the question of the
place of English study in the school curriculum, and of the
spirit in which that study should be carried on. If pupils of
average ability leave school without having acquired some
taste for reading and at least a rudimentary power of discriminating between gold and dross, of knowing what they
like and why they admire it, their school days have been

largely mis-spent. The task is difficult, but it is not impossible. In the larger centres of population children are fortunate, as a rule, in having access to abundance of reading material, and it is the duty as it is increasingly the practice of teachers to guide the pupils in their selecting of books. In country districts, until quite recently, libraries were the exception, and as the ordinary home in rural areas has no books as part of its equipment, pupils had nothing to read except the contents of the school library supplied by the generosity of Mr Coats many years ago, and worn literally to tatters. Nowadays the Carnegie Rural Library Scheme is performing a service of incalculable benefit in every area of Scotland where authorities were wise enough to avail themselves of the admirable facilities offered by the Carnegie Trust. I have been informed time and again by teachers how eagerly the pupils anticipate the pleasure of choosing and perusing the books that are circulated. I lay stress on the word choosing, because in my own parish I have had experience of the working of a library on the Open Access System. Too long have their elders told the youngsters what to read. Within limits that need not be specified meantime, children should read what most appeals to them. Every classroom of every school should have its own book-shelves, not locked but available at all times of the day, and every parish should have " live " books. That will solve some difficult problems. A mind well-stored is less easily tempted.

English Literature must, of course, be the principal item on the card, but I venture to make a plea for the conservation and perpetuation of the Vernacular. I have always advocated and practised its study in school, and it is to be hoped that Scots classics will soon be more readily available than they are at present, so that all pupils in school will have the opportunity of learning to familiarise themselves in written form with the language which many of them speak out of school. Why should not all " Reading Books " have selections of Scots prose and verse? The chief hope, however, for the Vernacular lies in its being studied by adolescents and adults in Continuation Schools and Classes, Literary and other Societies. Almost every county has its own particular literature in Scots. My own county has "Johnny Gibb" and "Life among my Ain Folk "; George Macdonald; Charles Murray, in addition to a wealth of ballads and other folk-song so lovingly collected by Gavin Greig. And Burns, Scott, Galt, Barrie, McLaren, and others are national possessions, waiting to be used for individual reading, social study, musical interpretation and dramatic representation, as means of profit, delight, instruction.

The place which the Vernacular holds in other parts of Scotland is occupied in the Highlands by Gaelic. In spite of— it may be because of—fourteen years' sojourn in Inverness-shire, I cannot say that I can honestly support all the claims that are made by Gaelic enthusiasts, the more perfervid of whom propose to establish training centres for Highland teachers, after short notice to insist that non-Gaelic-speaking teachers shall find employment elsewhere, to make Gaelic teaching compulsory whether parents wish their children to receive such instruction or not. Such proposals as these are not only destined to prove abortive, but they do incalculable damage to a cause which is worthy of support. Gaelic should be taught where it is still spoken if parents and pupils desire it. As in the case of Scots, its preservation and extension must depend on the intelligent and discriminating interest of those whose heritage it is. Compulsory study will never help to perpetuate either Gaelic or Scots. The sane enthusiasts in this matter are those who encourage the holding of Musical Festivals and the formation of associations for the promotion of correct speaking of verse and of prose.

If, as I have tried to show, there is a distinctly rural problem in connection with the cultivation of the native literature, the native language, its dialects and substitutes, the case is very much stronger so far as concerns Mathematics and cognate subjects. No educational change of the last thirty years is more symptomatic than the fact that in all save the most conservative circles "Euclid" has been dethroned from his seemingly impregnable seat. His "sequence" was no doubt the best that he could devise, and may still be admirable for "pure" mathematicians, but it is by no means suited to modern requirements. A generally agreed on sequence of geometrical propositions is not only advisable but necessary, if mathematical teaching is to be carried out on natural lines, but, as in every other branch of Science, the order and emphasis should be susceptible of modification and adaptation. The same is true of the syllabus of Algebra and that of Arithmetic. The treatment of each department must, of course, be on strictly logical lines in all schools, but in country districts Arithmetic should have a distinctly rural basis. Pupils do their best when they are interested. They are interested in that with which they come daily in contact. How many of the " tables " in Arithmetic could be more easily learned in the playground if we could get rid of the notion of " drill " and substitute the practice of interesting play! Every school should have a garden, and each class should have its allotted portion of the garden. Then it would be possible to have real nature study with abundance of suggestions for all kinds of problems in observation, experiment, calculation, artistic and graphical exercises. Get rid of the urban notion of Science teaching with its continual emphasis on the mechanical " dead " side of Science. Take the wonderful world about as starting point and returning point—the fields with their rotation of crops, trees, garden, dairy, poultry, bees. Study chemistry not in relation to its power as a destructive agent, but as a help in every beneficent operation. All about us in the country is material for real scientific study without the need for recourse to expensive apparatus. The most suitable, the most effective apparatus for the teaching of rural Science is that which is made on the premises if there is a close co-ordination of the Mathematical, Scientific and Bench work; which, in most rural schools, is not only possible but also compulsory. Every article made in the woodwork room should be directly usable in school or out of it. And Cookery lessons for country girls, and boys, should be concerned at least as much with the preparation, the food values, the dainty serving and the economical use of such ordinary country fare as can be cooked without a range or even a Perfection Cooker, as with " higher-class " cooking.

It is a matter of experience that a well-planned course of Practical Work has a marked effect on the intellectual development of dull pupils. Let us not wait till the pupil has " qualified " before we let him use his hands. All about us in the country are models and suggestions. Reading, writing, arithmetic will be better, not worse done if the toil of learning them is frequently relieved by the singing of a

Scotch song, by " making " something of interest and utility, or even by a merry game out of doors. Only those who know of the facility which the country offers for the realisation of such reasonable conception of training understand that the country is the best place for education. There is, indeed, a specifically rural problem. Not for nothing did the Lord place Adam in a garden. A sandpit is a more educative place for a natural child than a cement " playground."

LANGUAGE STUDY, WITH SPECIAL REFERENCE TO LATIN AND GREEK.

FOR the last ten or twelve years the utilitarian conception of education has been in the ascendant. We have prided ourselves on our scientific attainments. So far as advance in science has added to the national well-being and has not been used for unworthy ends, there is good ground for satisfaction. Yet it is to be feared that many who exalt the position and potentialities of science on the ground that it is thoroughly "practical," and who at the same time decry the study of literature, especially the literatures of Greece and Rome, know very little about either science or literature. It is generally admitted that the study of English is important and valuable, at least as far as it increases, or is likely to promote, subsequent material success. Thankful for even this modicum of interest, we are hopeful that a nobler conception of the value of a love of literature as a permanent possession will become more widespread as a result of the efforts now being made through the influence of education and the institution of circulating libraries to popularise knowledge.

The person who puts in a plea for greater attention to the study of Latin and Greek must expect to find comparatively little encouragement in a utilitarian age, especially when ruthless economy, without regard to the consequences so far as the other fellow is concerned, is the popular cry. There can, however, be no doubt that the Greek and Latin classics have real and substantial claims to an increased share of attention. We shall not try to defend the study of these subjects on the ground that they have been for centuries, and still are to some extent, a principal component in the education of those who have had a large share in making and keeping our Empire great.   An instrument so powerful and tested through such a long period cannot be lightly discarded for some untried tool.

Much of the prejudice against the classics has its root in the fairly common belief that for many years they occupied a privileged position, and it must be admitted that formerly Latin and Greek had an advantage over such subjects as Modern Languages, for no Arts degree could be taken without including Latin and Greek.   For the last thirty years these subjects have not been compulsory in the Arts course, though one of them at least is still required for the Arts preliminary examination.   In their own interests and for the sake of classical study, both in graduate and post-graduate education, the University authorities should not insist on a pass in Latin as a qualification for entrance to study for a degree in Arts. It is always inadvisable to put any subject except the native language, which should be compulsory in every Arts course, in a privileged position.   The claims of Latin and Greek are so intrinsically strong that, given a fair field and with their claims properly advanced and supported by a reasonable allocation of bursaries to deserving students who mean to specialise in them, they will not fail to attract those who wish to study for honours in any branch of literature, history, or philosophy.

The Latin and Greek Classics have an exceedingly strong claim to be admitted to a prominent place in the curriculum of higher schools.   A very considerable part of modern civilisation is based on and springs out of the ideas of the Greek and Roman civilisation.   Many of the institutions of existing society are modelled on those of Greece and Rome. Much even of our practice springs from the activities of these nations.   Our fundamental ideas of law, the greater part of our systems of philosophy, mental, moral, political, and other, are based on the principles that inspired and regulated the thought and action of the nations whose influence was so far-extending and so permanent.   Our literature is indebted to Greek and Latin for inspiration, for suggestion, and even for specific matter.   These and similar grounds are not matter of sentiment or personal opinion.   The study of the Classics does not need defence or apology on such a narrow basis. Such study should never be championed except on the absolute merit of the languages themselves. Give the Classics a reasonable chance to be studied by pupils during the years when their memories and powers of retention are keenest, and the application and attention thus bestowed will be rewarded even from the narrow, more utilitarian point of view. English literature has one great advantage over Greek and Latin. In range, in actual content, and in execution, English stands unrivalled, and no one can say that it may not yet be carried to even greater perfection than it has hitherto attained. The total of Greek and Latin writings is, on the other hand, completed. But the value of the Classics is very great from the fact that nearly every form that is found in modern literature can be paralleled in the great Classical writers. Moreover, the problems of thought and of practice that engaged the minds of the Greeks and Romans were those that press for solution in the twentieth century. In trying to solve these problems, we have the advantage over them that we can trace the whole of their systems and behaviour right to the end, and are thus able to judge how far the principles and methods they made use of were calculated to and actually did enable them to attain the projected goal, how far at times they failed. They had to work to some extent in the dark, having no precedent to guide them.

Problems of world wars and their immediate and more remote effects, of imperial responsibility, of rural depopulation, and of doles, of the strength and limitations of democracy in peace and in war engaged their attention as they absorb ours. We can, if we will, learn by their experience, the experience of those who in the realm of thought and of its successful application to the actual problems of life have up to the present time had no superiors.

It is the fashion in certain " superior " circles to despise what is called " mere memory," but a little reflection will prove that this faculty is an element essential for success in almost every department of business and professional activity. The popularity, often it must be admitted as temporary as it is widely advertised, of systems of memory-training shows that many people have learned by experience that a bad memory is a serious handicap and that they think it worth while spending time and money to try to remedy the defect. The learning of Latin and Greek declensions is in my experience one of the finest methods of training and increasing the memory power, but I do not approve of confining pupils to these for several weeks and months at the beginning of their course. Here, as elsewhere in education and in life, the principal point is to create and maintain interest. The learning of foreign languages can be a very dreary process unless all the available aids are employed from the first. Luckily there is now an abundance of texts which are suitable for beginners to read aloud, and I have found that this combination of grammar—the pupil learning only a little every day—and reading aloud, with very gradual introduction of translation, produces very quick and sound results. The use of maps and of mythology and the giving of the relevant historical and geographical setting make of the Latin lesson a time quite as interesting and instructive as is possible or advisable where serious work is concerned.

In the Perse School, Cambridge, the headmaster, Dr Rouse, and his colleagues have for several years carried on the teaching of Latin and Greek by what is called the " Direct Method," that is, in the same way as modern foreign languages are usually taught. For a considerable period at the beginning of his course the pupil employs the language as a spoken tongue, the material for conversation being found in the ordinary surroundings of school and of home. An attempt is made—and at the Perse School apparently with great success—by dialogues, the telling of stories, the acting of plays, &c., to secure the active interest and co-operation of all the pupils. Translation is not required nor even encouraged till the pupil has been for a considerable time learning the language. The rules of grammar are not taught formally, and the reading of classical authors is taken up comparatively late. Translation from English into Latin and Greek receives very little attention at any stage, but the pupils are encouraged to write original essays in the foreign tongue. This method has not, at least in anything like its entirety, become acclimatised in Scotland, where the grammatical tradition seems to have become difficult to supplant.

I agree that " dead " languages, which are, by the way, very much alive on most of the deeper and more permanent problems of life, cannot be taught entirely on the same lines as, say, French. The subjects with which the Classics principally concern themselves forbid absolute similarity of treatment, but my experience has proved that "gerund-grinding" in the learning of Latin and Greek has been seriously overdone. If from the very start the lesson is based on the work which the pupils actually read aloud with due attention to rhythm and quantity, and if grammatical *essentials* are learned more or less as they are required, progress in the learning will be both rapid and sure, because interest will not flag. The teaching of the Classics may thus be and often is vitalised. We must try ever to remember that the ancients were men of like passions with ourselves, and not mere expositors of the rules of syntax and of grammar. Direct questioning in Greek and Latin I have not found permanently valuable, but the Perse method suggests a point of view that is worth considering.

Latin is a logical language most carefully elaborated. It has, of course, what may be called the normal arrangements of words, but owing to its retaining practically all its inflections it can vary this arrangement almost without any restriction. In this way it can bring out shades of meaning and secure emphasis for some particular word or phrase to an extent that is quite impossible in any modern language usually taught in schools, though German retains the power in some degree. From the beginning of his study, therefore, the pupil must give attention to careful analysis and examination of every word and even of every ending. The habit of exact observation is thus cultivated, and the logical faculty is evoked quite as strenuously as in the tackling of a mathematical problem. In the early stages it is not, of course, possible to dwell much on the securing of emphasis by the change in the order of words, but very soon that appeals to the inquiring child, and one is surprised to find how much this adaptation of means to the promotion of ends is appreciated by the pupil who has something of the artistic faculty.

In my opinion, it is advisable to go slowly in introducing the pupil to the mysteries of the "version." Latin is a difficult language, though it is only fair to say that it can be made less or more hard by the use or abuse of various alleviations. Very educative work can be done in learning this language for six or even more months without making the path too thorny by strewing it with the briers that abound in Latin prose composition. But when the fitting time comes, there is, in my opinion, no better test of a pupil's powers, no finer means of training the reasoning faculty than the attempt and the ability to write Latin prose. Even moderate success requires the possession and the use of considerable acumen. The scholar must set himself to understand the setting of the passage of English to be translated, to analyse it clause by clause and phrase by phrase. He has to compare the methods of expression in the two languages, to consider fine shades of meaning, figures of speech and idioms. A knowledge of Latin phrases, a sense for style, and the selection, as model of an author whose style will suit the particular passage to be translated, all these are essential preliminaries.

The question as to which foreign language should be taken first by pupils in school is not easily answered. On the grounds that it is modern, useful, and supposed to be easy, French has of late years been prime favourite with the majority of pupils in ordinary higher grade schools; but it can hardly be denied that from the scientific point of view, Latin, being the parent language, French should be studied, not before, but after Latin. In any case, the scholar who is going to study Latin thoroughly should begin about the age of eleven or twelve, and start Greek about a year later. The languages are in their genius and structure so much akin that the learning of the second is comparatively easy if the study of the former has been thorough, and progress is much more rapid. Greek is fortunate in having an abundance of literary matter which the pupil finds easy and interesting even at the very early stages of his study, and pupils not intending to specialise or even to graduate in the language, have greatly benefited by even a two years' course begun after they had studied Latin for three years.

The question is sometimes asked—" Is it worth while to acquire a reading knowledge of a language without troubling about all the minutiae of grammar and composition? " I am by no means in favour of " soft options," but if a student has been thoroughly disciplined by the study of Latin and has thus acquired the sense for language, he will without any doubt derive immediate profit and permanent pleasure by learning to read Greek classics. We stipulate, however, that such study must go hand in hand with regular and systematic attention to Greek mythology, literature, history and art. On whatever principle Greek is studied, it should, like English Literature, be taken in great swaths. It is too nervous, too artistic, to be subjected to dissection and pedantic criticism.

It should be at once admitted that for the study and appreciation of English literature and language it is not by any means necessary to study any other language, ancient or modern. Many enjoy these treasures who have had no formal school or college training, and can express themselves as correctly and convincingly as others who may have learned several tongues. But experience shows that the influence of the study of Latin on the pupil who wishes to become a real student of English is very considerable. From the point of view of language alone, English is more indebted to Latin than to any other language. Quite one-third of English words are derived from Latin, and even a short study of Latin pursued with interest and energy assists the pupil immensely with derivation and, therefore, with the understanding of English words, and gives him an immediate and striking advantage over the non-Latin pupil.

In my own experience the Latin scholar is in almost every case the best English scholar. He brings from Latin to the study of his native language a training in exactness, in clear thinking, in lucid statement, and in the power of observation and discrimination that seems to put him in possession of a master key. Our age is a very practical one, and it is necessary to go straight for one's objective, but even shrewd business men have proved and admit that what they find most useful in their assistants, and especially in the higher ranks of these, is not so much a training in technical subjects at schools as a broad general education based on systematic study of English, Latin, and other languages, with, of course, adequate and even liberal attention to mathematics and science.

The question of the influence of the study of Latin on the learning of French and German is so much akin to the problem already considered in connection with the study of Greek and of English that it is not necessary to deal with the matter in detail. I do not entirely agree with the opinion which is at present fashionable that French is the easiest foreign language for pupils to begin with. There is a superficial resemblance between English and French, for example, in the order of words and in the absence of inflections, that seems to induce the belief that the difficulties to be faced in learning French are much less serious than those presented by Latin. Yet in Scottish schools there is hardly any subject where there are so many failures as in French; which is almost certainly not due to any want of zeal or ability or knowledge on the part of most teachers of the subject. French *seems* an easy language; but as a first foreign language it is comparatively difficult. To study it first seems an inversion of the natural order. Study Latin first, and the difficulties of French in its earlier stages will largely vanish. Progress will then be almost incredibly rapid—the pupil will learn as much in six months as he would have learned in eighteen without a previous course in Latin—and the study of advanced French, very hard in my opinion without Latin, will become both rational, because based on logical and scientific principles, and free from difficulties that are otherwise very formidable to the average student.

Over twenty years' daily teaching of German at all stages to pupils who have, and to others who have not studied Latin has convinced me that the genius of the German language is so akin to that of Latin (and to a less extent to that of Greek) that the successful study of German is facilitated to an almost incredible extent by a previous course in Latin. As in the case of English, I do not at all assert that Latin is an essential preliminary for success, for I have had some few non-Latin pupils who were very competent German scholars, but the effort entailed is so reduced and the mastery attained over the language is so pronounced and enhanced in the case of the pupil who has studied Latin that the layman would with difficulty be convinced that such a difference is possible.

Should pupils begin the study of Latin who are to leave school before they can advance far? That depends entirely on the kind of pupil under consideration. If home influence and his general outlook tend to turn his thoughts continually away from culture towards actual employment, blind-alley or other, a pupil will do little or no good work at school, whatever subject he may be set to study. If, on the other hand, he understands that he is at school for a definite purpose, to prepare for living, there is no reason why he should not benefit immensely by even one year's study of Latin. Again, it is objected that everything that is to be learned from the study of the Classics can be got from translations. This is simply not the case. In the first place the discipline that is secured from language study, which is of unrivalled value, cannot be got from reading translations. These have a certain value for those who cannot read the original; but even in the best translation much is lost. Atmosphere cannot be translated. Beauty lies not only in the ideas, but also in the order of words, their rhythm and the metres. Figures of speech cannot always be translated.

Not a great deal may be lost in translating certain kinds of prose—for example, history and certain parts of philosophy —but the great speeches of Demosthenes and Cicero rendered into good English are but pale shadows of the originals, and great poetry, the epic of Homer, the drama of Æschylus, the Eclogues of Virgil defy the translator's skill. Dryden's " translation " of Chaucer and of Shakespeare into " modern English " made even Dryden appear ridiculous. Charles Murray, with all his genius for the writing of Scotch poetry, can hardly be congratulated on his rendering of Horace into the northern dialect. " A man may make a good English poem with the matter and thoughts of Dante, may even try to produce their metre or rhyme; but the metre and rhyme will be in truth his own, and the effect will be his, not the effect of Homer or Dante "—(Arnold). The objection that the Classics are useless because no one now speaks them hardly deserves notice. In these loud times there are more important things than speaking and, after all, there are plenty of languages for colloquial use.

It is said that we live in a scientific age, and that there is no time for ornament. The Classics are by no means merely ornamental, and in any case the opposition between the Classical and the Scientific schools is now nearly obsolete. Both sides were seriously to blame, for they were each con- temptuous of the other, and they both fought shadows. We are becoming wiser, and are finding that co-operation and mutual respect are both more conducive to general progress and more becoming in those whose aims should be the same.

EXAMINATIONS.

THE subject of this chapter is so acutely controversial that I think it advisable at the outset to state my general attitude on the question. I believe in examinations, because I believe that this is a moral world, and that testing is an essential element in progress. The question of examination in educational work in no way differs from the testing of any other kind of work. How is work tested in any department of activity? In all cases the success of the operation is tested by the actual work of the day. In every relation of life this holds good, for the present and for the future.

In educational discussions and organisation much attention is given to what is called the normal pupil. The phrase is a handy one to denote the possession of abilities that are neither very far below nor much above those of the average individual; but a much more precise classification is needed if the best results are to be secured, and we seem to be on the eve of an era of real scientific advance in connection with the study of experimental psychology. Binet's intelligence tests have now been used long enough to prove that they can be relied upon as means of measuring intelligence, and of giving reliable help in classifying pupils. Experiment proves that children differ enormously in endowment, and it is both unwise and uneconomical to try to make all follow a uniform course at the same rate of speed. Wherever possible, special arrangements should be made for the education of those who are distinctly sub-normal, in the interests of themselves and of others. But the present examination system is specially detrimental to pupils of outstanding ability, who are often delayed in their course simply because of their age. Wherever the use of intelligence tests shows that the pupil of, say, ten years of age has the intelligence of a pupil of twelve, he should be at once promoted, so that he may not fall into trifling ways but may have his mental powers fully occupied and trained with a view to his becoming a leader in some department of activity.

From the passing of the Education Act in 1872 to about the end of the century, the system of external examinations might almost have been said to run riot in Scotland. Every pupil at practically every stage was examined by outsiders, and passed or failed as an individual. The final estimate of the year's work depended on the result of an external examination lasting one day or less. No matter how efficient the pupil might be in the opinion of those who taught him during all the other days of the year, he was denied promotion if he failed on the testing day. Teachers' prospects and pay were strictly in proportion to the number of passes and failures. The utmost effort was exerted to secure a clean sheet of passes, not only that the wolf might be kept from the teacher's door, but also in order to avoid parochial disgrace, for these were the days when the intelligence of the managers was equal to counting the number of failures and discussing them in the talking centre of the community. These were the bad old times, when pupils were prepared, not for the business of life, but to pass a ridiculous test, in order, ostensibly, to prevent the country's money from being squandered. No one was more conscious of the absurdity of the system than the parochial schoolmaster, but he was part of the machine, and he had to try to adapt himself to his surroundings.

New packs of cards (of the arithmetical kind) were bought and worked through by every member of the class, each question on the card differing only in some slight detail from the corresponding question on every other card. The subjects set for English composition, the questions asked in history, geography, analysis, and parsing by the inspector were, not by wireless, but by methods not less reliable, communicated by the teacher whose pupils had just been tortured, to the unfortunate victims in the neighbouring parishes. These tests were worked out time after time by teacher and pupils until the examiner arrived and wondered that his method of examination had been so intelligently anticipated. The schoolroom received its once-a-year scrubbing, and smelt strongly of soft soap. That soft soap was typical of the whole bad system. It was not a question of how you lived and taught and learned day by day, of trying to develop personality, of getting to know a little of the glories of literature and nature and art, but of being " scrubbed " for the only day in the year that really counted, in order to make a decent appearance and to avoid being looked upon as a failure, and to enable you to obtain the bare necessaries of life. All the time you knew that you were the unwilling accomplice in depriving the bairns of their birthright. You might have made your pupils "letter perfect" for the day of the inspection; you knew that it was rather manipulation than education. It is easy to be a mechanic, it is difficult to inspire.

Some still sigh for the reintroduction of these methods of barbarism, but they have no children of their own at school and no real knowledge of the work that goes on in schools conducted on rational lines. They know nothing of the natural outbudding of the child's nature. They are ever restless to pull up the plant to see how it is growing.

No one who has the knowledge and experience sufficient to enable him to judge will claim that education has suffered by the partial freedom that has come from the elimination of the cast-iron method of written examinations at every stage. Some hold that there should be no external examination at all, and show the sincerity of their conviction by sending their children to schools which are not subject to any outside test. Although they have to pay fees at the selected school, they hope at least that the work of instruction will be carried out on reasonable lines. To advocate the general adoption of this plan may seem a counsel of perfection in present economic and social conditions; but there is no doubt that it is in harmony with the ideals of Plato and Pestalozzi, who were not altogether fools.

For—and I know that I am myself speaking for many experienced teachers—I hold that for the average pupil examination is necessary, but the examination should be internal and should be conducted by the teachers concerned, aided and supervised by the headmaster and by H.M. Inspectors who have gone through all grades of teaching. All good schools have regular tests on the work done, set partly by the teacher and partly by the headmaster, and carefully adapted to the age and capacity of the pupil. The results of these tests are carefully tabulated, and taken in conjunction with the pupil's performance of his daily work in *every* subject of the course, form the only reasonable basis for forming a considered judgment as to the pupil's attainments and claim to promotion. Tests by outsiders should be almost, if not wholly, oral until pupils have reached the age of fourteen or fifteen, and always conducted in presence of, or preferably by, the class teacher.

When the time for promotion arrives, it is of the utmost value to get the reasoned opinions, based on work actually accomplished, of all the responsible teachers, who know that they are *really* responsible. With these opinions recorded and backed by the actual work of the pupils during a whole term, it is possible to arrive by conference and discussion among those concerned at a result which experience has proved superior to that obtained by any system of external control. I strongly advocate the establishment of a Consultative Board in areas of reasonable size, whose duties would include the fixing of standards, the giving of guidance and advice, the deciding of doubtful cases, and generally the co-ordinating of the work of schools. The Board established in Aberdeenshire for this purpose has now been three years in operation, and the results have abundantly justified the hopes entertained by those who proposed it. The standard of Qualifying work in the county has been considerably raised in almost every school where an improvement was reasonably possible. Appreciating the freedom and responsibility that they know by experience belongs to them, teachers are successfully striving to educate more and cram less. Conference between those who have taught and those who are going to teach certain pupils will, if both sets of teachers are resolved to plan for each pupil the course that will best enable him to realise himself, produce a result which has not yet been attained by the examination system hitherto in vogue.

Even the Civil Service Commissioners have begun to realise the importance of oral examination and of the personal interview, and they have to deal, not with immature minds, but with those who have gone through a full secondary school course and in many cases have taken a University degree. If the external written examination has proved unsatisfactory as a means of discriminating between grown-up candidates in an open competition, it is surely high time that it were dropped where the task is merely to promote pupils to a higher class without any thought of competition or material gain.

The evil effects of external written examinations on the health of young pupils, and especially of girls in their teens, are too patent to require comment. Preparation for these is the most potent means of keeping girls from spending more of what should be their spare time out of doors, where they would learn much more that would be of permanent value to them if they were not obsessed by the nightmare of unnecessary tests. In the interests of sound education of mind and of body, all those who have seen the evil effects of examination in the case of their own children will do their utmost still further to break the shackles that bound all pupils and still fetter too many pupils of tender years.

This sensible system is now in operation in a few areas in Scotland, but what is euphemistically called a Control Test is still too prevalent. This consists usually of questions in English and Arithmetic, with the addition of others in History, Geography and what is called General Intelligence, in certain counties.

In spite of what its apologists say, this system of promotion is inherently unsound, even when consideration is given to the recorded opinion of the responsible teachers. Why examine only in English and Arithmetic? The obvious and only answer is that these subjects alone are capable of mechanical measurement. Because the result of the teaching can be thus tested, these subjects are specially taught with a view to success in the examination. Other subjects which are quite as important as these for all pupils, and much more important for certain pupils, come insensibly and quite unconsciously, so far as the responsible teachers are concerned, to be looked upon as of comparatively small importance. Instead of being free to co-ordinate the subjects of the curriculum and to let the children feel that they are engaged in a high adventure, teachers are compelled to divide the hours of the week and the day into water-tight compartments and to concentrate on what will pay. Complaints are often made that too many people live with an eye on the main chance. Are the schools free from reproach in this matter? It is impossible to compress children's minds day by day into a cramped mechanical system without producing permanent effects for evil. A school is not a factory. It should not be a training ground for people of the "ca-canny" type who imagine that responsibility for work is over when it has passed the test. A very alarming result was recently shown in one county by the application of an external Qualifying Examination. Sixty-eight per cent. of the pupils qualified normally, that is about the age of twelve. Ten per cent. qualified late. Twenty-two per cent. were *unqualifiable*. This last statement would be most serious, if it were not so absurd. It is a slander to say that one-fifth of the pupils in a county are not mentally able to proceed to the next stage. The teaching is presumably efficient; the children are probably pretty much like the children in other counties. The fault must lie with the methods or the standard of examination.

Unfortunately these Control examinations are being used for a purpose that is even less defensible, in fact quite illegitimate and unworthy. If a pupil gains a certain percentage of marks, say 75, in such an examination, he is selected for admission to a secondary school. A smaller percentage secures his entrance to a higher grade school with a three years' course comprising at least one foreign language in addition to English, Mathematics, Science and Drawing. Advanced Divisions, which may mean much or little according to the conditions under which they are carried on, are the lot of those whose marks place them in the third category. Those rated still lower are ordained to stay in their own schools, which usually implies that though they have scraped through this illogical test no special provision is thought necessary for them. And yet their parents are compelled to pay their share of the expense; the pupils themselves have faculties that may indeed differ from those of the seventy-five per cent. members of the class, but which are by no means negligible. Last of this mechanically assorted company appear those pronounced "unqualifiable," marked and branded in the eyes of others and, much worse, in their own eyes as failures, fatally handicapped at the outset of their "career," almost inevitably condemned to the ranks of the inefficient. It is difficult to write with moderation about such a ridiculous travesty of a system which is an absolute contradiction of every principle of modern child psychology and of ordinary common-sense, not to speak of justice. We pride ourselves in living in the twentieth century. Such practices are unworthy even of the dark ages. We are sinning against the light. Let us cease trying to fit the child to the mechanical system. Let us devise courses to suit the varying capacities that God has made or that human injustice or depravity has produced.

The awarding of school bursaries to pupils on the results of these external Control Examinations is entirely indefensible. The money used for this purpose comes out of the pockets of all ratepayers without distinction. Such money should be given solely on two grounds, capacity and necessity. Capacity includes not merely intellectual acumen and superficial smartness such as can be tested by a written test, but staying power, outlook, sociability, in short, what is known as character. Necessity is difficult to define in the minds of some parents who apply for bursaries for their children. Administrators need have no difficulty in the matter if they get the necessary information from reliable sources.

Such Control Examinations entail considerable expense. One Scottish county spent five hundred pounds in conducting such examinations in one year. The reader will be able to calculate how many bursaries of ten pounds each that sum would have provided for pupils who could have been certified by their teachers, if they were capable, fearless and worthy of their position, to possess the qualities required for continued study, and in whose case even such moderate financial aid would have been a real incentive to more advanced study.

A Government Department is not given to boasting and presumably cares nothing for praise or censure, but the Scottish Education Department has in the last few years proved its faith in the matter of responsibility for promotion by its works. In no unmistakable terms it has intimated that such responsibility lies mainly with the teachers concerned, those who have taught and those who are going to teach the pupils. After the experiment the Department has found it possible to assign increasing importance to the duly-formed, considered judgment of the responsible teachers in the award of Certificates, while, of course, it retains the power to deal with cases where negligence, inefficiency or incapacity is proved. If the teaching profession will purge itself of petty personal jealousies and assume reasonable responsibility in a spirit of mutual confidence, it will make possible an immense advance in Scottish education.

The days of the purely external examination as the sole or even principal means of judging the success of any department of work are surely numbered. Examiners are, therefore, now expected and almost without exception are glad to fill a more reasonable, more possible role—to be fellow-workers with the teacher. Only in the final school examination, for pupils of the average age of seventeen, is the knowledge of individual pupils tested by written papers prepared outside the school, and even in this case success or failure is not finally fixed until pupil and responsible examiner are brought into personal touch in the presence of the teacher. Teachers appreciate the striking advance that has been gained by continuous sapping and mining. Their ideals and efforts and accomplishments in this connection should be regarded with approval by University Professors, who have always retained in their own hands the examination of their students, with, of course, the assistance and collaboration of an external examiner selected by the University Authorities and not imposed from without. The teaching profession asks that this sensible and tried system be applied to the testing of school work at every stage; and at the point of transference from school to University they will welcome the co-operation of the Universities in sifting the unfit from the qualified. In making this demand for limited autonomy the schools realise that they are taking on their shoulders a considerable responsibility, but they are convinced that the new circumstances require it—a fresh orientation. Its collective experience and the research it has conducted in this connection have impressed on the profession some very definite conclusions, which can at present be stated only very summarily. External examinations are not a reliable method of testing fitness or of finding out the qualties that are necessary for University study and for solid success in after life. They may gauge and assess powers of memory, superficial smartness and the capacity to reproduce at short notice what has been " packed " by an experienced teacher who has studied the art of selecting what will pay. The more elusive but far more valuable qualities of trained ability, sane outlook and power to deal with new problems and unusual situations, external examinations will not discover. There are unworthy methods of mark catching as of vote catching, such as the working and re-working of tests previously set. It is a well-established fact that different examiners assign to the same answers widely differing marks, and that the same examiner unconsciously varies his standard with the length of time he has been engaged at the revision of some scores or hundreds of papers, and even from day to day according to the state of his health. To remove entirely the personal factor from the problem of marking is admittedly impossible, but no unprejudiced person will assert that the complaints made by examinees have no justification. Trained psychologists recognise increasingly that the traditional method has outlived its day. We must, if we are to do justice in the future, lay stress on the daily work accomplished by the pupil or student periodically tested by oral and written examinations conducted by sympathetic and experienced experts able to make skilful use of Intelligence Tests. So long as the present system is allowed to continue of carrying on education by *over-specialisation with a view to success in examinations* and the holding back of pupils so as to gain a spectacular triumph with detriment to those who are thus retarded and discouragement to those whose parents cannot afford the additional expenditure, real educational progress will be impossible. There may be very much testing and a perfect riot of examination with very little education. There is considerable ground for the allegation that the average adolescent does not know how to read and use books, and still more for the charge that only a moiety are really capable of acquiring such knowledge for themselves after their school days. Enlightened teachers fully recognise the justice of the claim made by the Daltonians. It is only what the pupil does that educates him. Owing to an absurd over-estimate of the value of examinations, our class-rooms have become far too much listening rooms where virtue consists in assimilation with a view to verbatim and even literatim reproduction. If knowledge is to grow, if wisdom is to get any chance, every schoolroom will become increasingly a laboratory, a scene of *childlike activity* and inquisitiveness where the natural spirit of romance and wonder will not be blighted by artificial standards of judgment.

IS THERE TOO MUCH TEACHING?

THE statement is frequently made that teachers as a class are exceedingly conservative, that the habit of mind and outlook of a considerable proportion of them are static, and that they look coldly on proposals that are calculated to bring about reform or even reasonable progress. The charge thus made may not be wholly accurate, but that it contains a considerable modicum of truth no one who lives much with teachers will deny. There is no danger that teachers as a profession will become revolutionaries, and on the whole, perhaps, it is well that they are not too radical. Of this conservative outlook and attitude there is a comparatively easy explanation. The profession has for ages been accustomed to " acceptance " rather than to " suggestion." Until quite recently the whole course of their training tended to keep teachers in the path of tradition. Only in 1918 did our legislators think of giving teachers any effective voice in the administrative side of Scottish education. It may be also that teachers have unconsciously lived and acted in such a way as to deserve to some extent the reproach of being unduly moderate. The mere force of habit has no doubt also operated to induce them to follow the old course rather than to try experiments that might be disturbing to their peace of mind and their prospects.

Yet there are among teachers an increasing number of enthusiasts for reform, some of whom, it may be, deserve the name of revolutionaries—a name, after all, not necessarily suggestive of anything very dangerous. The revolutionary of one age is often looked upon as a mild reformer or even as a reactionary by the next. We need only mention Rousseau, Froebel, Dr Montessori, the Dalton Plan, The Project Way, McMunn, Neil, to show that not all teachers are content to jog along in the old ruts, and undoubtedly there are many others who, though they have not the gift of originality, are willing to reduce new theories to the test of practice. Some at least of the theories are not entirely new. They merely re-state principles once widely accepted by teachers or lay stress on aspects that have come to be over-looked.

Hitherto the " class " system has been general, and it has advantages; for example, those that arise from sympathy of numbers, emulation, the inspiration that comes to the teacher from a large class, the fact that it seems to be economical, though in all probability the result will be more an illusory than a real economy. In spite of the virtues, real or supposed, of the class system, all who know the school from the inside are sensible of the limitations and drawbacks that attach to a method of classification in accordance with which a whole class of pupils follows the same prescribed programme.

Some drawbacks of the class system may be briefly men-tioned. The relation existing between teacher and pupil is built on a bad foundation. It really takes from the pupil a responsibility which he should at least share, and that in-creasingly from year to year, and lets him throw it entirely on the teacher. The teacher's business is to arrange the work for every minute, to see that done, to watch for slackers—with doubtful results. The relation is essentially wrong. The pupil ought at least to co-operate in the plan if not in the method, to become more or less responsible for the actual working of the scheme. This feeling of responsi-bility is to be inculcated not only as a training for what is called the actual business of life, but even more in the interest of the pupil's own immediate welfare and real progress. Pupils, like other people, are always more methodical, more diligent, more prudent and provident, as well as more efficient, when they are really made to feel their responsibility. The class method of instruction, rigidly applied, is apt to breed dependence and court resistance.

Under the class system it is assumed that all pupils can make the same, or nearly the same, progress. This is certainly not the case. It may be questioned if there is even an average pace at which, say, 60 per cent. of pupils can travel with comfort and safety. There are pupils who can advance much more quickly. These are retarded, discouraged, and, being impelled to find an outlet for their energies, break rules, disturb others or dream away their precious time. Slow pupils, on the other hand, become confused and perplexed. They are compelled to simulate an interest in the work of the class, but are unable to follow the instruction with intelligence and therefore with profit. They gradually develop a dislike for school, a distaste for learning, and are classed, it may be quite unjustifiably, among the failures.

A pupil may be very clever at one subject, say English, and rather backward at another,—*e.g.*, Mathematics. The class system makes no allowance for such an idiosyncracy. Such a pupil must spend at the study of English all the time that the other members of his class give to that subject, and get no more time for Mathematics than the others who may excel in it. The same restriction applies to all the members of the class with their varying tastes and aptitudes. This allocation of a pupil's time is unnatural, unfair and calculated to defeat the end in view.

The class system makes it difficult for pupils who have been compulsorily absent, or transferred, or promoted, to join the appropriate class without serious loss. The inevitable result is that such pupils become " backward," uninterested, dull, duller, despairing and despaired of.

If a pupil is weak in one or two subjects he is retarded and loses a year. In theory, of course, a pupil who is weak in a subject may be transferred to a lower class during the period appointed for instruction in that subject, but difficulties connected with organisation as a rule prevent this, and the path of less disturbance of the Time Table is followed, with results discouraging to the pupil.

The drawbacks thus baldly stated seem obvious. Why have they been allowed to persist?

The class system is cheap, at least on the surface. Expenditure on education has always been more grudged by the public than that on any other service. Most people pay lip-service to the value of education; only a small proportion believe in it and are willing to pay for it—which, after all, is the best test of the sincerity of conviction. (A witty writer has suggested to the advocates of the League of Nations and organisations with kindred aims that they should agitate for

8

the placing of all expenditure on Armies, Navies and Air Forces on the rates. The result would be interesting and the plan perfectly effective if the proposed reform were extended to all lands.)

There is much ignorance of the conditions that actually prevail in school and of what is meant by education. A pretty general notion prevails that educating boys means keeping them in order, and that the best teacher is he who most resembles a drill sergeant. In this connection we are reminded of the old hero who could keep such "good" discipline that "you could hear a pin fall." It may have been "discipline." It had nothing to do with education. Education is not herding, but training beings who, however alike superficially, differ almost indefinitely physically, morally, emotionally. They are the creatures, as we all are, of heredity, of home circumstances, of associations, less responsible therefore than mass-production theorists are inclined to allow.

Habit counts for much. "That which has been must be." Parents were themselves educated under the class system, they have heard of no other; they are contented to let things go on as before. Only here and there do we find a parent who is progressive in this matter, and he (or more often she) has proved by experience that defects exist which should be repaired.

Teachers are conservative by training and outlook. They fall into ruts and remain there. Like others, they love the limelight, like to rule their little kingdom, to be the centre towards which all choose, or are compelled, to gravitate. They like to have the last word.

Lecturing is so much easier than educating, getting into touch with the pupil's mind, envisaging the problem from his point of view, engaging in give-and-take by questioning and allowing himself to be questioned by the pupils.

But there have been questionings and investigation and research. Experiments have been made, and as a result of these definite proposals of reform have been formulated and published. The earliest of these in quite modern times is linked with the name of Dr Montessori, who began a crusade against what she regarded as an indefensible system. Those who were responsible for the Education Acts of 1870 and

1872 were like all pioneers and enthusiasts in this respect that they did not realise the possibilities and the liabilities of the system which they introduced. If they had foreseen even a moiety of the social, economic and political changes that were to follow inevitably upon the passing of legislation for compulsory education, they would probably have held their hand, knowing that public opinion would not have backed them. One result of the decision to educate all children over five years of age was that the individuality of the child was lost sight of. Stress was laid not on the child but on children. Pupils were therefore massed in large classes numbering as many as eighty or more. During part of the school day the teacher in charge might have the assistance of a pupil-teacher; as a rule she was left to do her best with this big assortment of little folk. These were the days when stress was laid on such phrases as sympathy of numbers, the firm hand, strict discipline.

Dr Montessori convinced herself that this herding together of a large number of young pupils in a class was psychologically and essentially unsound. She laid stress on the individuality of each child. She insisted that the child, not the class, must be the unit, that the school should cease to be a place for mass-training, simultaneous action, superimposed guidance, and should become a sphere of individual initiative, of intermingled play and work, of self-suggested mutual helpfulness. So far as the teacher was concerned, her function was entirely transformed. She was no longer to teach or instruct, but to become a directress, not imposing her will but, where necessary, encouraging the little members of the Republic to try experiments with the abundant toys, tools and other requisites for self realisation that the normal child loves and can use for its own pleasure and development. Dr Montessori brought us back to first principles, and in that way did a great service to education. The seed she sowed has produced a rich harvest. Her system has been adopted with extraordinary success not only in Infant Departments, but in other divisions of schools. Best of all she has made teachers think and examine themselves, and the methods which, alas, they are too apt to look upon as sacrosanct. Her influence has stirred and inspired others to investigate and try experiments, and everyone who knows anything about education has heard of such " new-fangled " notions as The Play Way, The Project Method, Free Discipline.

One of the most interesting and promising of these recent proposals is the Dalton Plan, which takes its name from the American town where it was first practised in 1920. Its advocates claim that the plan is entirely new, though some people are of opinion that in essence at least it has been compulsorily used for many years in schools where more than one class is habitually taught, or at anyrate directed, by one teacher. A short sketch will enable the reader to grasp the main features of the plan and to estimate the possibilities of success that it offers.

The feature of the plan that seems most novel and striking is that the pupil is made responsible for carrying out the work appointed, allocating the time allowed as seems best to himself, and for the progress he makes. Parenthetically it may be remarked that he is not responsible for choosing the subjects of his study unless he has a very indulgent, rich and perhaps sensible parent. The time for allowing such choice of subjects may perhaps come, but external tests will first have to be abolished, the influence of traditional and conventional standards of judging education will have to be destroyed, so that a man's value will be estimated by what he *is* instead of by what he is supposed to know.

The pupil must convince himself, or be convinced, that the mere fact that the teacher is paid for teaching is not enough, that the work of education is his own concern, that his success or failure must depend primarily upon himself, on his own initiative, diligence and other qualities.

If he is thus responsible, the pupil must have large freedom to arrange the terms and manner of his work, to select suitable apparatus, books of all kinds and companions as co-operators. Naturally the pupils will select those who are like-minded and sympathetic, who like the same subjects or subjects for which their tastes and aptitudes differ. In such co-operation there are certain latent dangers which may bring disaster unless due care is taken. One pupil may do all or most of the work, while the other is passive; but this can be easily discovered and prevented. There is the risk of premature specialisation and of lop-sidedness when co-operating pupils carry Division of Labour so far that each of the partners always confines himself to his own favourite section of the task in hand. In such a case it is plainly the duty of the teacher to see that there is such an interchange of function that each pupil understands all the underlying principles involved.

The pupil must have access to qualified and sympathetic teachers when he find that he needs assistance. He must be allowed to work under suitable conditions and have at his command at least as much apparatus as is found in the best modern, well-equipped schools.

The essential elements of the plan, which is not a definite, fixed system, may be briefly summarised. For each subject of the pupil's course the teacher (or teachers) plan the work to be accomplished in a given time, say a month. This is called the assignment. For the study of each subject a room (or part of one) is set apart. These rooms are provided with all the apparatus, including the text books, books of reference, charts, maps, models, tools, scientific equipment, and so on, which the pupil needs. In each room, which in reality is more like a laboratory, is the teacher of the subject, who might more fittingly be called the consultant or adviser or director.

The main responsibility lying on the pupil, he has the utmost freedom. He may study one subject for an hour, a day, a week as he pleases. He may begin with what is for him an easy subject, leaving the more difficult till later on, or vice-versa. He may work by himself or in collaboration with his fellows. He may consult the adviser if he wishes. The only restrictive condition is that he is expected to cover the assignment within the given period, unless, indeed, it is found in the case of individual pupils that they can do more satisfactory work by confining themselves to part of the assignment appointed for normal students.

The function of the teacher in the working of the Dalton method is to a considerable extent modified. He has to draw up the monthly assignments and to be ready to give necessary assistance to individual pupils (or to groups) when asked as to any detail or difficulty.

It is his duty to secure that all books and apparatus are used with due regard for their purpose, and so that each student has reasonable facilities for study. He has to see that the atmosphere of his laboratory is one which permits the pupils to study with profit. The ideal is to secure that the laboratory be a hive of industry, each pupil being engaged at his individual or co-operative work. There should be no suggestion of the barrack room or of a Quakers' meeting-house.

Theoretically, there is no reason why the "Dalton System" should not be used to the entire exclusion of the "class" arrangement, the pupils being engaged the whole day at individual work, with the modifications already mentioned. In practice, however, the Plan is used only to a modified extent. In some cases the whole forenoon is devoted to "free" work; the afternoon is allotted to class work of the traditional type. In other cases a smaller proportion of time is given to individual study, the major part being given to formal teaching. Certain schools have adopted the Plan in their senior classes, with the intention of extending it downwards if it turns out well. There seems to be an inversion of the logical order in such a practice. If Montessori methods, original or modified, are suited to the Infant Room, it seems most reasonable that some adaptation or extension of these methods should be employed for some time after children have left the Infant Room, and that the Dalton Plan should be used in all the other Divisions, instead of the more rigid class system.

The Plan, which had its birth in America, has been carried on in a large number of schools of different grades, Secondary, Boys', Girls', both abroad and at home. Teachers who have adopted the Plan in whole or in part have met to compare experiences, and the following results and advantages appear to have accrued from its adoption.

The progress made by each individual pupil is more sound than that secured by the class system, based as it is on what he himself has done or experienced. "It is only what the pupil does that educates him." By using the Dalton Plan the pupil becomes an active, responsible agent working conscientiously towards a definite goal along a course every stage of which he has traversed for himself and is not a mere receptacle of a homœopathic dose of learning prepared and administered by an outsider.

An undoubted weakness of the class system is that the pupil does not learn to use books for himself. Even successful teachers are much given to preparing elaborate notes which, in some cases at least, are " dictated " to the pupils and thereafter learned up for reproduction, it may be, at examination time. The average pupil therefore leaves school without having received any sound training in the individual use of books. The Dalton Plan postulates initiative and inquisitiveness on the part of the student.

The pupil is no longer driven at a speed which is uncomfortable to his mental, and even physical equipment, and certainly destructive of his chance of making sound and solid progress. He can allocate his time according to the difficulty which he personally experiences in each branch, devoting more time to what is for him hard, less to what is easy.

The time being definitely fixed and the assignment, the student has to solve his own individual problem of looking at the work as a whole and overtaking it in the way that will best consort with his own tastes and capacity, and therefore with the prospect of the most enduring success. There is no interruption of interest at the end of a " period." The pupil who becomes absorbed in some problem, literary, scientific, social, artistic, is free to continue his study until he has satisfied his interest or exhausted his immediate store of energy.

If the object of school education is, as it must be on any reasonable hypothesis, to prepare the pupil for living as opposed to making a living, the Plan has much to recommend it. The pupil is trained to accept a gradually increasing responsibility. He has to organise his abilities so as to produce the best possible result in the given time. He thus gets to know that in work there is not only meaning but dignity and satisfaction. The Plan makes him understand from the first that the only real, solid education is self-education, reared on the foundation well and truly laid by previous students who have left the results of their devotion to study in the treasuries of books, scientific knowledge, artistic accomplishment and other riches now at the command of whosoever will. The Plan is calculated to produce a sounder relationship between the pupil and the teacher, each being enabled to understand better the point of view and difficulties of the other. An absent pupil is not discouraged, for, on his return, he can resume where he left off. A new pupil can join at any time without suffering retardation in his work. The student who is backward at one subject and has failed to cover the whole of his contract in one year does not require to retraverse all the journey of the previous year—he can go straight forward with the subjects that he has mastered.

It is a disputed point whether the Plan makes the arrangement of a curriculum simpler. Some hold that it is easier to plan for a single individual than under the class system, but if an assignment has to be made out for each individual pupil the inference is not obvious, indeed, the conclusion is, in my opinion, not warranted.

From the point of view of expense, the Daltonians hold that their plan has the advantage inasmuch as it is not necessary to provide as many copies of a book as there are members in a class, seeing that only a proportion of the pupils, say one-half or one-third or one-sixth, will probably be engaged simultaneously at any particular study. The same applies to apparatus, so that the equipment which is so essential to the pupil's progress can be more complete and more varied. In this connection one sees more than a prospect of relief for the oppressed parent who, being compelled to transfer his children from one school to another on change of residence, has to meet heavy charges for new sets of books. Another common ground of complaint is said to be removed by the adoption of the Dalton Plan. The assignment is planned in such a way that the pupil can with reasonable diligence cover all the work within school hours. If he cares to devote some of his spare time to extending his knowledge beyond the limits prescribed, he is, of course, at liberty to browse at will, but the advocates of the plan rather discourage such enthusiasm, preferring that the students should cultivate other interests, that they should, for example, train and develop the social sense. If prescribed homework can really be abolished or even sensibly diminished by the plan, we have no hesitation in saying that it will deserve well of parents, pupils, teachers and society. But so long as external examinations are tolerated, not to say idolised, one has grave doubts as to the possibility of securing this much desiderated reform.

The acccommodation at present provided for the class system might be sufficient for the carrying on of the Dalton Plan for a time, but the large amount of individual work that is required by the plan would undoubtedly render extensions imperative. All rooms would really become laboratories, and the amount of extension required can be readily calculated after comparison of an ordinary class-room with a room for practical instruction.

No one will accuse the present age of holding exaggerated views as to the place and value of discipline. It may be, indeed we are sure it was the case, that the average school thirty years ago was rather a stern, forbidding place, in which repression and prohibition played a much greater part than suggestion and encouragement. But the modern school, if it is not exactly a place of delights, is on the whole a scene of wholesome, happy activity. The Daltonians affirm that they have solved the problem of school discipline. Feeling that the job is his own, that the responsibility for its success is not only not assumed by another, but is consciously and deliberately devolved on himself, having his interest awakened and his enthusiasm stirred, the pupil is convinced that it does not pay to waste his own time, much less to be mischievous and troublesome to his fellows. This standpoint is at the opposite pole from that of the boy (actually existing) who freely asserts that " school laws are made to be broken," and who, when he is multiplied even by a relatively small digit, proves a constant source of vexation and a disturbing element.

What happens to the pupil who has not completed his assignment? In the first place the assignment is carefully planned so that it can be carried out by an average pupil in the time allowed. It contains matter which it is essential that the pupil should master before he proceeds to the next stage. But it also suggests " side lines " and extensions which may be followed up by those whose inclination or enthusiasm or prospective needs urge them in that direction. Some of those who have worked the plan prefer the making of different assignments to suit varying capacities to having graded assignments of the kind just mentioned. For those students who find particular difficulties in any subject, recourse to his fellow-students is both permitted and encouraged, subject, of course, to his satisfying the teacher that he has personally mastered the allotted task. The advice and help of the teacher are also available at all times during the free hours, so that individual pupils or a group of pupils can at once be guided round an awkward corner. Again, it must be remembered that in most institutions that have adopted the plan, a greater or less proportion of the time is devoted to the class system with its opportunities for collective investigation, demonstration, questioning, testing and revising. By such means as these, the residue of the unfit and unadaptable pupils is reduced to very small dimensions. In this category will be found the pupil with a " twist." He is a problem for the psychologist with his mental intelligence and other standards of measurement. If, after due trial, a boy does abuse the liberty which is an essential feature of the plan, he must be deprived of that freedom in part or in whole. His spare time must be curtailed so that he may devote his attention to a definite task prescribed after the method of the class system. Few pupils will hold out long against a well-thought-out and carefully sustained plan by which summer evenings and Saturdays are commandeered in order that they may do what they deliberately have left undone. Some teachers are in favour of depriving the " slacker " of games, music, eurythmics, art instruction, school journeys and similar " reliefs." Such a plan might be effective with some natures. There is, however, a type of boy for whom it would have no terrors and mean no real deprivation. He would only be urged to become more of an actual boor and of a potential danger to society.

With regard to expense, it has been found that the new plan does not require more teachers than the class system. The teacher, however, plays a new part. He is freed from the perplexing problem of drawing up a class Time Table. He is relieved of the burden of preparing lectures, notes of lessons, epitomes, digests, which are supposed to contain in short compass all the information that it is necessary or wise for the pupils to " get up." He has to assume the more difficult, the more testing role of planner and adviser. Having made the Assignment, he stands to some extent aside and leaves the pupils to " try themselves." From being the pursuer he becomes the pursued. He becomes the adviser and co-operator instead of being the keeper of the conscience and the dictator. He must become a different and a *better* teacher, for, without making any hollow pretence to be omniscient, he must be prepared not to examine but to be examined and cross-questioned and puzzled as only young people with eager minds can puzzle. So in all likelihood greater expense must be incurred in order to provide a more extensive, though not less broad-based education for future teachers.

Much time spent by the teacher at correction of pupils' exercises under the present system is wasted. No part of the teacher's task is more arduous; none is less appreciated by the pupil or has less influence on him, apart as he usually is from the teacher during the process of correction, and feeling himself free to stow away the corrected exercise as quickly as possible, unscanned. Under the Dalton Plan the corrections are made by the teacher in the pupil's presence, or better, by the pupil under the teacher's guidance. Such individual work with individual pupils, impossible under the class system, is within limits quite feasible with the Dalton Plan.

Daltonian enthusiasts find themselves confronted by an obstacle that has often blocked the path of the reforming teacher. I refer to examinations. It is possible to write a theoretical defence of examinations, even of external examinations, if the estimate of education is founded on a mechanical basis. But external examinations have proved themselves the dead hand that has *nullified* or *retarded* the realisation of the ideals of all educational reformers. We have gone some considerable way in the direction of abolishing them; we must not rest till we have completed the demolition of the hateful structure. Internal examinations are advisable and necessary, the natures of teacher and pupil being what they are. Even these, however, must be regarded as *tests of study*, not of education. Now a monthly assignment seems, *prima facie*, to necessitate a monthly examination if the teacher is to be sure that each pupil is qualified to tackle the next assignment. So the early Dalton enthusiasts set elaborate examination questions, which entailed equally elaborate note-taking and committing to memory on the part of the pupils and laid upon the teacher a burden of correction under which the conscientious among them were literally overwhelmed. Experience teaches, and now practice has shown what common-sense revealed long ago, that short informal tests, oral and written, are quite sufficient, particularly if supplemented by term examinations say twice a year.

I do not favour the practice of substituting the methods of
the popular debating society for the regular and systematic
study of English, but the discussion of short papers written
by pupils from various points of view, and debates conducted
with the conscious aim to educate and not merely amuse
might, in my opinion, be more effective than elaborate
written examinations, and at the same time stimulate the
pupils to prepare themselves for the discussion and decision
in later life of questions relating to local and national affairs.
Whatever plan or system, or modification of these, is adopted,
teachers and others need to be reminded that the first and
main purpose of a school is to educate.

The average text-book, written as it is largely from the
point of view of the teacher, is quite unsuited to the carrying
out of the principles of the Dalton Plan. New books are
needed based on modern rational conceptions of education and
on the results established by experience and psychological
research.   Luckily, existing reference books are good and
available at reasonable cost.

One of the proverbs of the wise is, " There is nothing new
under the sun." Like many other popular sayings which
unthinking people accept at their face value, this saw has
enough truth in its favour to make it pass muster. We are
surrounded by many inventions and discoveries that are indeed
new, and the world is destined in the near future to see many
new developments, both beneficial and detrimental to human
progress. But the Dalton Plan is not entirely new in educational practice. It is merely a modification of the system that
prevailed in the old parish school where the teacher, in most
cases, had under his charge several classes at various stages
of advancement, and in certain instances taught or tried to
teach pupils from the Infant Class to the University Bursary
Competition standard. The cost at which this feat was
accomplished cannot be calculated at present. The tale is a
painful one from the point of view of the teacher, the taught,
and the not-taught—the last-mentioned being by far the larger
number. And the plan is still compulsorily in operation to a
greater or less extent in every primary school where all the
instruction is carried out by one, two, three, four or any
number of teachers smaller than the number of classes.
Teachers of one class have their own problems and trials and

must do a great deal of hard work. If they could exchange places with the teacher of a small school, containing pupils of every age from five to fourteen, they would admit that there are compensations for having to teach sixty pupils, supposedly at least all about the same stage of advancement.

As has been indicated, a rather acute controversy has been carried on as to whether the Dalton Plan differs essentially from the system that has prevailed for many years in smaller schools with only one, two or three teachers. No doubt there are features in Daltonianism that were not found in the practice of the small schools in former days. These did not possess the facilities and equipment for the many different branches of education and instruction that modern conceptions and demands render imperative, and on which the advocates of the Dalton Plan insist. All the same, while it may be admitted that the two systems have more points of difference than of agreement, those who have taught as many as four or five classes simultaneously may at least claim that they have gained by experience much that the supporters of this new system urge on theoretical grounds. The writer can claim that for over thirty years he really, though not nominally, carried on the advanced departments of his schools on principles closely allied to those of the Dalton Plan, and he is sure that very much can be said in its favour so far as the pupil's sense of responsibility and self-reliance are concerned. The results may not be so immediate or easily measured by mechanical standards, but they are likely to appear to much greater advantage during the pupil's career in the wider school of life.

SUPER-NORMAL AND SUB-NORMAL
PUPILS.

THE super-normal boy was the delight of the parish schoolmaster's heart. And the much-longed-for pupil did appear at fairly constant intervals. As the future welfare of the country depends, to a considerable extent at least, on discovering and utilising these superior intellects, it is pleasing to find that in the last twenty-five to thirty years their number in the parish school has been practically doubled. The modern representative of the old pedagogue was not easily converted to the belief that the girl genius could ever be equal to the clever boy, either in mental calibre or in staying power. The revolution is, however, complete. Visit the advanced departments of the average country school, and you will find that the female element largely predominates in numbers, and often in ability. Twenty years' experience has convinced the most sceptical that in mental capacity and perseverance the girl can quite hold her own with the best of the boys, while in conscientiousness and devotion to what she considers or is told is her duty, she surpasses the boys to an extent which at times tends to become excessive and, it may be, injurious to the interests of health and to considerations of the social and domestic amenities.

There still remain a few who have not been able to reconcile themselves to the idea that there are super-normals among women as often as among men, but facts are stubborn opponents, and even these survivals of a less enlightened age may be convinced of their error when they find an increasing number of women of genius filling University chairs as efficiently as some professors do. Even ultra-Conservative Cambridge opened her degress, if not her doors, at last. Alas! that some actions should be shorn of all gracefulness because they are performed too late!

It is an undoubted fact that in every school there are pupils who stand out from their fellows in intellectual ability. Not every child that comes to school with the reputation of being a genius or even clever is highly endowed. Parental affection is rather a dangerous guide in such matters. Precocity is not genius. A child who has had every advantage that good feeding and every kind of attention can confer and who, in particular, has not enjoyed the inestimable privilege of having corners rubbed off in the rough-and-tumble that is characteristic of a big young family, may be merely pert and entirely lacking in the more solid qualities that are essential for success in the best sense.

Experience proves that pupils of unusual ability, some of them boys and *girls* of outstanding genius, appear with pleasing regularity from practically every class of society, except where extreme poverty has effectively nipped the bud of genius before it was disclosed.

In such cases Nature may have been bounteous; reasonably sufficient nurture was denied. Some people are so fond of parading their so-called democratic preferences as to declare that nearly all Scottish geniuses have sprung from the humbler homes of the country. The claim is greatly exaggerated. The number coming from such beginnings is indeed remarkable and probably unique, but, as it has been the boast and the glory of Scottish education that it has recognised no division into primary and secondary, and that the laird's son and the parson's son sat side by side with the stone-mason's and the gamekeeper's on the school bench, so they have all from every rank and without distinction of class brought lustre to their native land.

Should, then, those pupils of superior ability receive special attention as regards their education? The answer is undoubtedly in the affirmative. They are, comparatively, few in number, and in times when there is by no means a surplus of capable men with powers highly developed by education and experience in responsible positions at home and abroad, we surely need to catch, train, and utilise all the genius that exists. Whether we are to advance or retrogress in the presence of the increasingly tense struggle that faces us in the economic and intellectual spheres must depend on our discovering and enlisting as large a number as possible of creative thinkers and leaders in philosophy, politics, science, and art in their various departments and developments.

Some advocate the removing of these super-normal pupils from the ordinary school as soon as they have proved themselves to possess outstanding ability, and maintain that they should be segregated in special schools or classes. Such a policy might be dangerous for the genius, and would almost certainly be undesirable from other points of view. After all, it is a salutary experience for those who can learn without effort to be brought into close contact with their fellows who have to toil painfully up the steep slope of knowledge. To understand early how to appreciate the difficulties that have to be surmounted by those who are less richly endowed is not a bad training for those who in the natural course of things may become leaders or directors or even virtual dictators.

In the earlier stages, at least, of school education it is in every way desirable that all kinds should grow together in the scholastic field. And the greater freedom of classification that is now possible in all schools, and actually in existence wherever enlightened and progressive minds are directing the running of the machine, makes this plan quite feasible. Thanks to the work of the educational pioneer, we have left behind us for ever the idea that the first and only basis of classification of school children must be the financial one. In well-organised schools clever pupils are promoted as soon and as often as advancement is considered desirable. Scholars of outstanding ability can and do overtake the seven years' course of the primary school with the utmost credit in five years, and that, too, without any damage to their physical health. Had they been retarded for any such insufficient reason as that their promotion would pick out the eyes of the class, they would have run the risk of falling into the habit of doing much less than their best. The danger in their case is not from over-pressure but from their having too few difficulties on which to exercise their powers.

Another very practical argument for the frequent promotion of pupils whose ability warrants it is that many parents cannot afford to keep their children at school till they are eighteen years of age. Many, indeed, must leave school as soon as possible after they have reached the age of fourteen, and it has been proved time and again that by careful attention to the problem of promotion in the primary school it became quite easy for the more highly-gifted scholars to gain the Intermediate Certificate a full year before the normal age of fifteen. The same holds true of the Group Leaving Certificate, and the saving of a year before a student proceeds to the University means a good deal even from the financial point of view. If the student has in view the gaining of a good Honours Degree and thereafter the prosecution of more advanced study, he should be encouraged to matriculate betimes.

A question hardly less important from the educational point of view and even more urgent from considerations of its economic and social consequences is that which concerns the sub-normal pupil. The country cannot any longer afford to neglect the claims of children of inferior endowment. No doubt differences of opinion may exist as to the proportion that these pupils bear to the number of normal children, but that they are sufficiently numerous to call for some kind of special consideration admits of no doubt. Such experiments as have already been conducted seem to place the number of sub-normals at about ten per cent. of the whole. This estimate is, in my opinion and experience, quite conservative, but it is better to err on the safe side and to make no over-elaborate changes until the actual position has been more definitely diagnosed.

Is there an increase in the number of pupils of less capacity? Probably there is not a larger proportion of these than existed thirty years ago, but nowadays there are more accurate standards of measurement, more scientific methods of observation and investigation, a greater readiness, or at least less disinclination, on the part of society generally and even of a moiety of parents to envisage the actual position and, if possible, to find a remedy. We have progressed far enough at least to make us cease throwing the blame on " providence," and admit that such influences as heredity, pre-natal conditions, environment and feeding play an important part. That the actual position is serious admits of no doubt. In a recent year 18,000 pupils in Scottish schools attained the age of fourteen without having even reached the qualifying stage. For them there was no entrance to any kind of higher education whatever. This state of matters is thoroughly unsatisfactory. It means that much time, energy and money have not been fully utilised. There has plainly been waste, and the blame lies at more than one door. Late entry, irregular attendance from various causes, migratory habits, are responsible for many cases of retardation, but there are other contributory causes, of which may be mentioned such as inefficient teaching, faulty organisation, excessive size of classes, mechanical systems of promotion. So long as promotion depends on external tests a considerable proportion of pupils will be penalised. From the Infant stage to the highest stage in Secondary Schools the only test for promotion that should be recognised is the fitness of the individual pupil to profit by the instruction provided for the next higher class, and the only persons to be satisfied on this point are those who have taught and those who are going to teach the pupils. Smart pupils should, as already indicated, be advanced as often and as soon as they are ready for promotion; normal pupils, as a rule, once a year. The residue will be found, as a rule, to comprise two categories, those who are slightly backward in one or two subjects, and those who are quite distinctly backward. For the former of these classes provision should be made wherever possible by the employment of supernumerary teachers who have been specially trained for this kind of work. By tactful management and by the use of modern methods based on sound views of psychology and of the influence of motor activity on intellectual development many of these pupils may be able to find their feet again, to join their classmates on almost equal terms and, best of all, to have preserved or had restored to them that self-respect that is such a big factor in securing success in after life. Where a school is not large enough to provide work for such a specialist teacher, the number of classes or of pupils under the charge of the ordinary teacher should be of such a size that a fair amount of individual attention can be given to the pupils who are less apt. The Dalton Plan affords very practical and useful help in the solving of this part of the problem.

More difficult to cater for are the pupils who are definitely dull, those whose Intelligence Quotient is under sixty. These pupils should never be grouped with normal children. As soon as the experienced educationist and Intelligence Test specialist have classified a pupil as " uneducable " in ordinary surroundings and by the usual school methods, special provision should be made for him.   More Central Institutions for such pupils are urgently required, and it is to be hoped that parents and Education Authorities will co-operate readily and even eagerly to give to the class of children referred to all the advantages that can be secured by the provision of specially-adapted accommodation with abundance of air-space and facilities for play-work.   Such an environment, supplemented by the services of teachers specially trained for the work after they have given proof of their ability in an ordinary school, has already been proved to produce very satisfactory results.   The curriculum must be very different indeed from that which was common twenty years ago and even from the programme of work that is carried out in an up-to-date school. Time Tables and similar mechanical devices must give place to free-and-easy methods adaptable to the needs of the moment.   The expense will naturally be much greater than would be entailed if these children were normal, but the future saving to the State even in hard cash, not to speak of the resultant advantage to society generally and to the individuals themselves, will prove to be more than worth the outlay.   In the larger centres of population such classes are already established, and even in less populous areas there are sufficient numbers of suitable pupils to warrant an extension of the system, especially now that motor-transport is available to bring children of the class under consideration from the surrounding districts.

One further step must be taken if the work thus accomplished is to produce a permanent effect.   In their own interest and that of the community such of the pupils as are proved by experience to be incapable of the self-restraint and regard for others that are essential to human progress and social evolution must be subjected to such forms of supervision and restriction as may be considered necessary.

RECRUITS FOR THE TEACHING PROFESSION.

EVERY army must have the gaps in its ranks filled up. The army which in the future is to carry on the battle against ignorance must be made and kept as efficient as possible if we are to retain our economic status in the time of increasing competition that lies ahead.

In view of the importance of the work of teaching, the strictest care in the selection of recruits for the profession is necessary. An increasing number of teachers will be required if the country is to do its duty toward its future citizens, but the quality of those selected is worthy of even greater consideration. I do not say that successful teachers have not already been or may not in future be drawn from every class of society, but there are certain strata from which it is hardly likely that suitable material can be extracted. The better ore you want the more careful will have to be your search.

In England up to quite recent times the educational standard for entrance to the teaching profession was very low so far as the ordinary teacher was concerned. In some cases the responsible authorities were said to be satisfied if the applicant had attained the age of eighteen and was in possession of a vaccination certificate.

In Scotland we have usually demanded some proof of education, not to say scholarship, from candidates for even the so-called lowest posts in school, and it is to be hoped that as the demands made on the teachers' education and judgment will be greater in the future a recognition of this fact will secure greater care in the preliminary selection of aspirants. You cannot make a silk purse without silk, and too great care and discrimination cannot be exercised by those who recommend and those who confirm the selection of applicants for training as teachers. The responsible are sometimes blamed for admitting to training those whose personality, outlook and ability fall short of the standard that is essential. Few will deny that there was a temptation to this at a time when there was a pronounced shortage of candidates, but the main responsibility will rest with those teachers who, owing to misplaced sympathy for the unworthy or from even less honourable motives, refrain from exercising the power of veto that is vested in them.

In addition to careful selection and regard for adequate educational attainments, it is necessary to insist on the successful completion of a course of practical training in teaching before applicants are admitted to the Training Centre. Only in this way can a reasonable guarantee be given that candidates for the teaching profession possess some aptitude for the work to which they are to devote themselves. There are few, if any, callings in which want of adaptability produces more regrettable failures than in the teaching world. To prevent misapprehension, it may be necessary to remark that the gifts that help to make a successful teacher in one department of school work differ from those that are essential for success in another. There are diversities of aptitude which, as far as possible, must be discovered and used where they will produce the greatest possible effect. But the idea that any one who has gone through a prescribed course of education can become a successful teacher in any adequate sense is fundamentally unsound.

In the securing of recruits for the profession these three points must be kept continually in view: (a) Teachers must be drawn from homes where the social, intellectual and moral atmosphere is wholesome; (b) their outlook on life should be cheerful and sympathetic; (c) the educational attainments of those seeking admission to the Training Centres must be high.

In this connection it is advisable to enter a strong caveat against the assumption often made and sometimes acted on that teachers with lower qualifications are quite capable of teaching pupils in the Infant and Junior divisions. The idea underlying this assumption is that the education of such pupils is less important than that of those in the Senior and post-Primary departments. On no ground of common-sense or of justice can the claim be maintained. The strength of a

chain depends on the strength of its weakest link. Lay a
bad foundation, build a weak course at an essential stage;
your structure will be unsound. There are more children
comparatively in the lower classes of a school than in the
upper. They are not less in need of the best education and
instruction; they are more rather than less eager to receive
these. It is not necessary to enter into the controversy as to
the comparative merits of men and women as teachers, for
as things now are it is becoming increasingly difficult to get
male teachers for primary school work; but if women are to
be the sole teachers of junior classes the qualifications held
by them must be as high, though they may be different, as are
demanded from men in other departments. After many years
of effort on the part of those interested in education, most of
the back-doors into the profession have been closed. The
holding of a Group Leaving Certificate is henceforward to
be the lowest educational qualification for admission to a
Training Centre, and the applicant must also have given
satisfactory proof of possessing those qualities that are
essential to the making of a satisfactory teacher. In the case
of males, admission to training will be open to those who
have taken a University Degree or the Diploma of a Central
Institution. The differentiation between men and women
in this matter is regrettable, at least on educational grounds,
but the increase in the numbers of women students who take a
University or Central Institution course encourages the hope
that within a reasonable time it will be possible to demand
the higher entrance qualification for all. No one who knows
the working of the schools from the inside will affirm that
a two years' course of academic and practical work in the
Training Centre is adequate to prepare a teacher for any
department. If the post-primary classes need the services of
highly qualified specialists, the pupils in the preparatory
departments, through which all must pass, are not less worthy
of the services of skilled teachers.

With reference to the time in the student's career at which
an attempt is to be made to discover whether she possesses
the qualities required to make a successful teacher, there is
a pretty general consensus of opinion among expert educationists that this should be deferred as long as possible, that
is, till the end of the Secondary Course, after the Leaving

Certificate has been gained. The existing Regulations allow a choice in this matter. The hours devoted to observation and practice in teaching may be spread over the last three years of post-Qualifying education or confined to the last year. The last thirty years has witnessed a complete change in the centre of gravity in this matter. The Pupil Teacher was a teacher first and a student only in name. She taught the whole day, and was herself taught before or after school hours or at odd moments. The Junior Student, as the name implies, was more of a student and very considerably less of a teacher, as she was not, at least she was not supposed to be, in charge of a class. (Many a Pupil Teacher was responsible for a large class; many others for several classes at one time.) In her case, however, there was a fatal fly in the ointment. The Junior Student was not compelled to gain the same Leaving Certificate as her fellow-students going forward to other professions. In too many cases she was satisfied, and her school was satisfied, if she escaped educational perdition by securing the Junior Student Certificate, which might connote very little indeed. I put in a very strong plea for deferring the period of observation and practice until the student's Secondary Course has been finished. No student can do justice to herself and her classes if she has to leave these to undertake teaching during part of the school day. There ought to be no premature segregation of pupils or premature choice of a future occupation on the part of a section of students. In the interests of *esprit de corps* and of the solidarity and comradeship of the learned professions, all should work together without the introduction of unnecessary distinctions. If a pupil makes up her mind at the age of fifteen that she is to become a teacher, and must therefore begin practical training, she may legitimately and even wisely change her mind, only to discover that she has wasted on teaching observation valuable time which her classmates have devoted to study. The teaching profession will never command the respect that is due to it if its members are to be branded at an early age. It is absurd to say that teachers should be satisfied with a lower standard of education than the members of other professions, which they must be if their attention is prematurely diverted from academic study. All students need to unite in study, in sport and in social intercourse without regard to their future vocation. As to the weaker vessels who " will never be good at examinations," they have their place. The nursery is a necessary and an honourable sphere. There ought also to be nursery schools. It is, moreover, contrary to probability and to experience to postulate that a woman is endowed with motherly qualities in inverse proportion to the amount of her intellectual endowment.

I am of opinion that the time is at hand when the teaching profession will have to face the problem of supplying specialist teachers in the primary school. The need for these is generally admitted for such subjects as music, art, nature-study; but a very cogent case can, in my opinion, be made for specialist teachers of English, of History, of Geography, and perhaps of all the other subjects, at least for pupils over ten years of age. Those who use their imagination to envisage the advance which the employment of such specially qualified teachers might secure will not consider a mere chimera the proposal that every future woman teacher (it is already required from men) should have gained a Degree or Diploma before being admitted to training. There is a certain amount of unreasonable prejudice against the demand on the ground that the possession of a University Degree is no guarantee of scholarship, much less of common-sense and other essential qualities. I agree. University authorities, however, are moving in the direction of securing that the M.A. Degree shall connote some definite standard of attainment. In the meantime there are several other degrees such as B.Sc., B.Com., LL.B., the holders of which are qualified to undertake necessary work in the educational common-wealth. That commonwealth needs also the services of those who have taken good diplomas at one or other of the Central Institutions whose reputation has been so greatly and deservedly enhanced in quite recent times.

It would, I am sure, be quite possible for these and similar institutions at home and abroad to provide suitable " refresher " courses for teachers who had given a certain number of years to actual teaching and who might desire to extend their knowledge and their usefulness. Expenditure wisely made on such courses and on the provision of facilities for travel at home and abroad would fully justify itself. The

League of the Empire has machinery in full working order to arrange Interchange of Teachers between the home-land and any of the Dominions across the seas.

No special help of a financial kind should be given to pupils on the ground that they are to become teachers. Such a policy is a kind of bare-faced bribery. If the parents of a pupil who has the necessary ability and the other qualities that are requisite to the making of a successful student require monetary assistance, such should be supplied without regard to his future sphere in life. A subsidised profession can never be a self-respecting or respected one.

Intending recruits are naturally and properly inquisitive and even critical about the immediate or more remote attractions offered by the career of teaching. They wish to have a guarantee that the conditions of their future work will be reasonably free from irksome restraints. They naturally expect to be allowed to do their work in an atmosphere of sympathetic appreciation. They hope to find scope for realising their ideals in accordance with the most modern conceptions of education without interference from inquisitive laymen and busybodies whose attitude is one of suspicion and distrust. They are quite willing to leave questions of external administration to be dealt with by those whose training and experience have qualified them for such work, but they hold rightly that problems of the relative place and importance of various subjects in the curriculum and of the methods of presenting these can be solved only by experts who have proved their capacity. Those who are looking forward to teaching have now comparatively little to be afraid of so far as external examination is concerned. The fight has been a stern one, carried on without intermission for over thirty years, but with the passing of the Qualifying Examination and the dropping of the Department's Intermediate Certificate examination the victory remains with the "moderns." Examinations in the form of reasonable tests, conducted by teachers and examiners in personal touch with the examinees, we shall always need and have, but in these there is no cause for trepidation on the part of the well-educated, hard-working, conscientious teacher who has ideals and the interests of the pupil at heart. Never again shall we tolerate what Sir Henry Craik, once looked upon as the high

priest of bureaucracy, called the " cruel ordeal " of individual
examination in the primary school. The modern examiner
is no longer an inquisitor, but a co-worker in the cause of
educational progress.

If the teaching profession is to attract a due proportion
of the best brains, financial considerations cannot be left out
of account. Reiterated assertions that teaching is the most
noble of all callings made by those who have little if any
experience of the work count for nothing. The profession
will never be entered by those whose first aim is to make
money. From that point of view it is almost the least
attractive. An inspector who had unique opportunities for
finding out the actual state of matters has put it on record
that the domestic economy of the average schoolhouse last
century was the last word in careful thrift. In every department of activity the monetary reward must bear some due
proportion to the amount of time, energy and money spent
in preparation. If material conditions in the teaching line
are on the whole inferior to those that obtain in other professions, the teaching ranks will be correspondingly attenu-
ated, filled by undesirables, or at least avoided by the better
qualified and more independent men and women. Almost
nothing is more galling to hard-working professional people
than the sense of insecurity, the feeling that a bargain will
not be kept, and nothing will more effectually deter suitable
recruits from joining the ranks than shabby treatment of the
older soldiers. The most effective recruiting sergeant is the
man who is in daily touch with the possible recruit and who,
being moderately satisfied and contented, will paint the
picture in attractive colours. Give fair, even generous terms
for first-rate qualifications and honest work. A discontented
profession in whose minds a sense of injustice is rankling,
is a positive if unconscious danger to a country, and it is not
possible to make the majority of the members of an admittedly
conservative profession discontented without serious pro-
vocation.

There is hardly any question connected with the conditions
under which teachers work that has been more clumsily
handled than that of superannuation allowances. Formerly
appointments were *ad vitam aut culpam*. Salaries were then
so small that teachers stuck to their work for years after

their powers were exhausted. Realising that this was from every point of view objectionable, the Department decreed that all teachers must retire on reaching the age of sixty-five. To provide the necessary retiring allowance, the amount of which was absurdly small, the teacher had to pay a certain percentage on his salary. Then, in a fit of generosity, the State itself provided the funds required to pay the premiums and compelled the teachers to take back the money which they had been contributing to make provision for their days of compulsory inactivity. Later, a system of compulsory contributions was again brought into force, and the Emmot Commission considered the whole question of contributory or non-contributory pensions, reporting in favour of the former, and a contributory scheme will be in force in 1926. Such vacillation has a very unsettling effect on the minds of the members of the profession, and is not calculated to produce a flow of recruits to the ranks. If a teacher's service is to be compulsorily terminated when he reaches a certain age, his salary during his years of work must be such that he can himself make provision for his old age or it is the duty of the State to make such provision. The same principle holds for break-down allowances.

Not every private soldier can become a field-marshal or even a brigadier-general, but all ranks should have definite grounds for expecting that promotion to higher posts will depend on scholarship, experience, proved capacity, meritorious service, and not on any fictitious or extraneous consideration.

Those who are responsible for the administration of Scottish education, and all who are interested in maintaining our country's educational tradition, are seriously perturbed at the dearth of male recruits for the teaching profession. The official statistics relating to the comparative numbers of men and women engaged in Scottish Primary Schools seem almost to justify the most pessimistic view of the actual position. In 1904 there were 56 men employed in Primary Schools for every 100 women. Every year since that time there has been a steady and accelerating decline in the proportion of male teachers, until in 1923 there were only 23 men to 100 women. The actual figures show that in 1923 Scottish Primary Schools had one male teacher to every five women, and that from 1904 to 1923 the number of men teachers fell from 4,549 to 3,801, while the number of women rose from 8,146 to 16,660.

Whatever views may be held as to the relative positions and value of the service of men and women in the general work of the commonwealth and on the vexed question of equal pay for equal work without regard to sex, there will be no difference of opinion as to the lamentable effects that must follow the threatened, and seemingly inevitable, disappearance of men from the ranks of Scottish teachers. Even if it be granted that women are at least as well qualified as men to teach and guide boys and girls up to the age of ten, all but the most doctrinaire feminist will admit that pupils beyond that age should be brought under the influence of male teachers at least for part of the school day. Further, it is generally admitted that in mixed schools the best tone and the best results are found where the staff is composed of men and women somewhat in the same proportion as the number of boys bears to the number of girls. A remedy for the dearth of male teachers is being sought. To find an effective remedy will be difficult, and the more difficult the longer it is in being found. What causes have produced or contributed to produce the existing dearth?

A suggested cause of the decrease is the change in the method of recruiting. Up to the end of the nineteenth century pupil-teachers played an important part on the scholastic stage. Boys and girls who were likely to prove apt teachers were enrolled as pupil-teachers at the age of fourteen or even earlier under the name of monitors. Many of them did not at all understand what immediate and more remote liabilities they were undertaking. Had they known what was expected of them in the way of teaching which lasted all the school day, and how little attention would be given to their own education, they would have hesitated. But their ignorance made it possible to staff schools with cheap labour, which was not always inefficient, and once started on a teaching career many of them continued and became excellent teachers. For many boys the pupil-teacher system supplied the only open road to learning and advancement, but the phenomenal progress of Secondary education, the demand for more highly educated teachers, the prospects and rewards held out by other professions, many of them unknown then, and other changes have made quite unthinkable any return to this method of finding recruits.

The Junior Student system which displaced the Pupil-Teacher never attracted a type of boy likely to be a good student and a successful teacher. Only a lad of little ambition could be induced to interrupt his Secondary Course in order to devote several hours a week to teaching when such interruption almost invariably meant that he could not hope at the end of his course to gain the Leaving Certificate which would admit him to University study and thus enable him to win a degree with all the material advantages and social prestige that a degree is supposed to secure. Boys naturally and properly despised a course which had most of the limitations and none of the advantages of the Pupil-Teacher system, and which was considered as successfully completed by the gaining of a Certificate that connoted very little. The Junior Student system must bear a large part of the blame for the alarming decline in the number of male teachers in recent years.

To an extent much greater than many people are willing to admit, the teaching profession is suffering from the unworthy treatment of teachers in the forty-five years that followed the Education Act of 1872. So far as remuneration is concerned, a typical case will be sufficient to establish the point. The fully-trained headmaster of a rural school noted over a wide area as a model institution so far as every detail of experimental and practical instruction is concerned, had to contrive to live and bring up a family on a salary that up to 1919 never exceeded £140 per annum. The status of the average male teacher was correspondingly low. His tenure was by no means secure, depending as it did in too many cases on his church connection, on party politics, and even on questions of merely parochial or personal significance. The treatment meted out to many teachers in these and similar ways has brought the profession into disrepute. A considerable proportion of the young men who might naturally be expected to enter the profession are the sons of schoolmasters, who grew up in daily contact with the stern realities of material, social and intellectual disabilities under which their parents travailed. The children avoid even the possibility of such experience, and choose professions where conditions are less forbidding. And their example is followed by their classfellows and companions, most of whom have been sufficiently in touch with the teacher's house and its economy, with his position and its insecurity, to keep them from placing their necks in the halter.

In spite of some amelioration of the teacher's lot in the course of recent years, the existing conditions are far from being attractive in the eyes of young men. They allege the comparative want of independence. They are of opinion that the amount of supervision is excessive, that in no other learned profession is so much time and money spent in the attempt to see that value is got for the outlay and that no slacking is prevalent. Payment by results is supposed to be abolished, but so far as the teacher is concerned it is said to be still in vigorous existence. The teacher who can bring the largest percentage of his pupils up to a high standard in an external examination, or who can secure the favour of some outsider who, it is alleged, is influenced by motives not calculated to promote the interests of real education is sure of promotion, especially if he is an expert in the use of unworthy methods of pushing his own claims. Too often promotion is said to fall to the man who has the most striking " paper " qualifications.

Salaries paid to male teachers of good qualification are alleged to be far too small to attract recruits. People with no higher academic qualifications, many with no University education at all, receive much bigger initial salaries in many departments of commercial life, and can reasonably look forward to conditions of service and of remuneration to which teachers of ability at least equal to that of their business contemporaries can never attain.

All these and other factors have undoubtedly contributed to the result that is so regrettable and that must become disastrous. The worst, however, has not yet been stated. Young men of good ability and self-respect will not enter a profession where they are expected to carry out a system which they have had no say in devising. Teaching has always been the Cinderella of the professions. There have been signs of concession and even of improvement in recent years, but the actual gains are not really substantial. Membership of School Management Committees, Provincial Committees and, worst of all, Advisory Committees, count for very little so long as the real power is in the hands of other bodies on which teachers have either no representatives or such a comparatively small representation that its influence in voting is negligible. Efficient, responsible teachers do not wish to encroach on the province of the administrator, local or national, but when questions of qualification, method, curricula and examination are being discussed, the representatives of teachers duly appointed by their professional organisations must be consulted, and their opinions must be allowed to carry great weight in the actual decisions. Even at the present time this reasonable system is not being carried out. Too often are conferences held to discuss subjects of primary importance in education at which representatives of all the governing and executive bodies concerned are present but no acting teacher has a place. This practice is not only vicious, but it inevitably produces a result absolutely fatal to educational progress. Teachers do not take a real interest in a system imposed from without. At the best they become the mere mechanical instruments of carrying out orders; in other cases they become unconscious and even dangerous critics of the system.

If a reasonable supply of male teachers is to be secured, the necessary steps must be initiated forthwith. The causes of the decline in their numbers are complex, and cannot therefore be removed without a very serious and prolonged effort. Improved material prospects must undoubtedly be offered. At least as important are the perfectly possible reforms that will make the teacher's position one of dignity, responsibility and reasonable freedom to carry out his own ideals in his work.

SCHOOL AND UNIVERSITY.
A PLEA FOR CLOSER CO-OPERATION.

ALL who realise the importance of education in the national life are anxious to maintain and even to raise the standard of advancement in the different subjects studied in Scottish schools. If this necessary result is to be attained, there must be a pooling of all the available resources, a determination to promote mutual comprehension and understanding. Of recent years there has been a certain attitude of aloofness, or, at anyrate, an absence of a good understanding between the Universities and the schools. As a result of this, certain desirable reforms have been postponed, among which may be mentioned more particularly the provision of an adequate supply of highly educated teachers. The time therefore seems opportune for putting forward a plea for closer co-operation between these institutions.

The reproach is sometimes cast at the Universities that they conduct their business proceedings too much in camera, that they live too remote from the world of school and business life. If such a charge could be to any appreciable extent substantiated, there would be much cause for regret. The more ordinary people are interested in the University, the better it will be for all concerned. So far as Bursaries and Entrance examinations are concerned, various parties have a close and immediate interest. Of these may be mentioned the pupils who are to compete and whose future intellectual progress and material comfort at the University depend to some extent on the Regulations which govern the conditions of examination. The parents also play an important part at that stage of the drama when questions of finance and maintenance fall to be considered. Teachers are legitimately and necessarily interested in these questions. They are responsible for drawing up curricula that will be adaptable to ever-changing circumstances and suited to meet the capacity, outlook and needs of various classes of pupils who may be looking forward to entering on any one of more than a dozen different spheres of activity, in addition to those who propose to study at the University. Teachers cannot make such arrangements satisfactorily, they cannot give that sound advice with regard to future courses and prospects that students have a right to expect, if they are kept in a state of uncertainty and perplexity such as has resulted in the last few years from the policy, or lack of policy, of the Universities' Entrance Board. Again, University requirements intimately concern the State, which, under modern conditions, is compelled to take close cognisance of educational efforts of every grade. It is the duty of the Education Department, acting directly or through duly accredited officers, to secure a certain minimum standard of attainment for the main body of the citizens of the State, which supplies the means of educating not as in former days a small, select proportion of the people, but all its members of varying capacity, different circumstances, various outlook. More and more, also, must the State concern itself with higher education of various types. What this country needs more than anything else in the intellectual sphere during the present and the coming years of stress and testing is a great development of educational activity that will provide abundant facilities for the training of adolescents. We need an immediate linking up of all the agencies that exist. The Universities, the State, all kinds of Institutions, statutory and voluntary, must co-operate, on equal terms and respecting their mutual autonomy, to secure provision for a great extension of education for adolescents and adults on voluntary lines, until the public conscience realises the seriousness of the problem of educational waste. Many people, therefore, are deeply concerned with University regulations; more will become interested in proportion as the Universities make themselves " popular " in the best sense.

The chief desideratum at the present time is that all who are really concerned for the progress of education should get together in a spirit of good-will—" there is no substitute for good-will "—with a view to setting the scholastic house in order. An essential condition of the success of this endeavour is a frank recognition of the fact that an enormous change in the educational situation has taken place in the last thirty years. Those are foolish and are merely courting disaster who persist in following an ostrich-like policy and in conveniently forgetting that the world moves with increasing acceleration every year. Proof of this may be found, if proof is necessary, in the modified conception of education in all departments of school work. Emphasis is now laid not on the education of a select few, but on training all young people as far as their ability warrants and the economic circumstances of the country allow. Up to twenty-five years ago many of the pupils, chiefly the brighter ones, were able to claim exemption from school attendance at the age of eleven or twelve. The master of a rural school could therefore devote much of his time and attention to the "lad o' pairts." Some regret the passing of those days, and assert that the system was justified both in theory and in results. According to these the majority of pupils are not worth educating beyond the most elementary stages, and the benefit accruing to the commonwealth and to the cause of learning by the concentration of attention on those of superior capacity far more than compensated for any loss sustained by pupils not highly endowed intellectually. Others, with equal emphasis, affirm that such a conception of education and such a practice are radically unsound. As a matter of mere historical fact the position is fundamentally and irrevocably changed. In our time regard must be had in school to the interests of the majority, whose bent is not literary, whose outlook is not scholastic in the narrow sense. Should such pupils be kept at school at all, is the question put by admirers of the ancient regime. To which we reply that they ought not to be in school unless a course of instruction suited to their capacity and outlook is provided at convenient centres; but on grounds of equity and even of the material welfare of the community, we cannot leave them and their claims to consideration out of account.

A transformation has been wrought in the course of instruction in Primary Schools. Formerly the three R's narrowly interpreted included the whole. Now the curriculum has been broadened and humanised to include such subjects as Drawing, Music, Physical Exercises, Hand and Eye Training, Domestic Science. The modern conception is generally allowed to be more reasonable and sounder on psychological grounds. School is a happier place and a busier. It may be that there is too much teaching, a defect which our Daltonian friends deserve our support in their attempt to remedy, but on the whole more really educative and effective work is done with and by the whole body of the pupils, though perhaps not so much of a narrowly intensive kind with the " clever." In any case, we live in a democratic age. We have deliberately adopted a policy of free, compulsory education as being not only reasonable but necessary. We have widened the franchise, and are about to extend the vote to what our grandfathers would have regarded as positively dangerous limits. All will admit that an ignorant democracy is an actual danger. We cannot now reverse the engines that we have deliberately constructed and set in motion.

A revolution has taken place in the courses of instruction in Higher Departments of schools. It is no exaggeration to say that till well on towards the close of the ninth decade of last century Latin and Greek were the main, and in some cases almost the only subjects taught in the upper classes of schools in which pupils were prepared for the University. One of my professional colleagues, himself a product of the famous Milne's Institution, a very high Bursar and one who rendered service of outstanding worth to the cause of education in the North-East, favoured me recently with a picturesque description of the Aberdeen Bursary Competition in his time. The gist of his remarks on Mathematics is " The Competition was limited to the first book of Euclid. Algebra was very elementary. Arithmetic was not extensive." It may be pointed out in passing, as illustrating the progress, or retrogression as some will have it, of education, that practically every pupil, boy or girl, of thirteen years of age in a properly organised school has overtaken a more extensive programme than the above in Mathematics. Practically all those who have completed their Secondary Course in schools are now able to pass an examination comprising Geometry, Algebra and Trigonometry on a relatively high standard, while in many schools the best pupils carry their studies much further in these and cognate subjects, such as Analytical Geometry. What, in my opinion, was even much more deplorable under the old conditions was the scandalous neglect of English, especially of English Literature. The study of English, so far as the Competition required, comprised (I quote my friend) "in one word, Bain's Grammar." I must refrain at present from elaborating my views on this state of matters. A system of education that regarded the glories of English Literature as of comparatively no account stood self-condemned. It may have produced men of metriculous accuracy, some of whom became very famous in various departments of activity. Their triumphs must have been won in spite of the fetters they were compelled to wear in their school days, and of their being denied time for access to the most wonderful literary realm and humanising influence that the world knows.

From the old curriculum Science was, except in a few cases, excluded. Pupils were sent into the world ignorant of the most elementary facts in connection with physical, chemical and biological Science. Drawing and appreciation of Art were neglected and even despised, to the permanent loss of those who were subjected to such deprivation of opportunity. Undisguised contempt was cast on every form of Handwork or manual occupation. Music, Singing, Eurythmics were taboo. French, German, Spanish were regarded as soft options. In spite of shortsighted opposition, all these subjects have established themselves more firmly because of the opposition. No one who knows school work from the inside, who recognises the place and value of these subjects when scientifically taught and their practical importance in after life as cultural, refining and social influences will wish to advocate that less attention be given to any one of them, much less to press for their exclusion. It is necessary to emphasise that a revolution has taken place, a revolution fraught with momentous and beneficial results to the whole conception and practice of higher work in the schools.

Not on merely scholastic or even narrowly educational grounds must the "new" subjects be recognised, retained and developed. The educational horizon of *all* countries has widened. We are faced with a new order in every part of the world. The East has re-awakened and is with increasing insistence demanding definite and substantial evidence of our right and our power to exact obedience or even to exercise sovereignty. All the circumstances and conditions, all the aspirations and needs of the century demand that we face facts. Surely educated people cannot close their ears to such an appeal. The introduction of these subjects into the school course has not only not lowered the general educational standard, but has raised it. Even if the standard of attainment had been lowered in the older subjects, which is not admitted, the greatly augmented breadth and extent of outlook would far more than compensate for a slightly lessened intensiveness. The correspondent to whom I have referred is strongly inclined to think that the older system produced a larger proportion of men who were able to gain scholarships at the English Universities, and that the schools do not now produce such a large proportion of " Big Men." The question is worth investigation and debate. It may be that distance lends enchantment to the view. In any case, conditions have changed. Those men were big enough to break the thralls of what may be regarded as a narrow course. More now even than then do we need men and women who are not merely scholars but people of broad mind and generous sympathies.

These changes affect the content of the curriculum, which has, as has been indicated, undergone an almost entire revolution. We have now to consider another important change. Prior to 1889 there was no Preliminary Examination for entrance on the ordinary four years' Arts Course at the University. The door was wide open to whosoever willed. Some are too young to know what the inevitable result was; others who had experience may have involuntarily or conveniently forgotten it; some, alas! remember only too well the cost that unrestricted entrance entailed. It may be conceded that some of the students who then entered on the first session of the four years' course in Arts were more intensively educated in certain subjects than the majority now are of those who begin the three years' course at the present day. A considerable proportion, on the other hand, were profoundly ignorant of anything more than the merest elements even of the Classics. In the year 1889, there were in Aberdeen University several students whose knowledge of Greek and Latin was less than rudimentary. The result was inevitable.

The whole standard of University teaching was lowered, because an attempt had to be made to teach in one class students who differed so vastly in attainment. The University was doing with wonderful success (I have never ceased to regard with admiration the extraordinary enthusiasm and devotion displayed by the Professor of Greek in the performance of his Herculean labour) work which should have been done in schools and which has in the interval been accomplished by the schools with increasing success as the unfit and the unworthy have been weeded out. The *average* pupil in a well-organised school is more advanced in the subjects then taught, and in some of the modern subjects also in addition, than the *average* student was thirty-five years ago at the end of his first University session. I do not say that education in Secondary Schools is as good as it might be, but it can face any reasonable comparison with the work of all save the best students in the junior University classes of the period referred to. Theoretically, the need for any examination-testing fitness to begin University study has to a large extent disappeared, and some may question if there would be much danger now in opening the doors to all who are willing to take upon their own shoulders the risk of failure. In practice, however, and with human nature what it is, it will probably be safer to guard the entrance door a little longer, in the interests of the entrants. All of which strengthens the present argument and plea for *much closer co-operation and a much better understanding* between the schools and the Universities. When these agree as to their respective functions and mutual relations, one more serious obstacle will be removed from the path that is supposed to be open from school to University. Meantime, anticipating what I have to say with regard to the Bursary Competition, I may be allowed to postulate that it is very desirable that the requirements for the Entrance Examination and those for the Bursary Competition should, as far as possible, be made uniform, and that with certain modifications the intending University student should, for the purpose of competing for a Bursary, be able to select the same subjects as satisfy the demands of the Preliminary Examination, and the same number of subjects.

A large percentage of pupils secure exemption from the

Preliminary Examination by earning Group Leaving Certificates at the end of their school course. At this point I
recognise how perilous it is to mention the Leaving Certificate, knowing as I do the regrettable absence of anything
like a good understanding on the part of the protagonists
on either side. It is well, however, to face facts and to realise
that there are two alternative ways of entering the University.
They are recognised by legal statute. Neither can abolish
the other. They will both continue to exist either as separate,
contending entities or, recognising the futility and the
harmfulness to important interests of their rivalries, their
supporters will become partners and co-operate with the
teachers and others interested in devising a *modus vivendi*
in harmony with their lofty mission.

I have no brief to defend the Education Department,
whose policy is sometimes denounced as autocratic. The
fault that most teachers have to find with the Department is
that it is too timid; that it keeps its finger too constantly on
the pulse of popular, and especially political, opinion; that
it follows rather than leads. I have never heard of its taking
a heroic step, which, after all, would be entirely unbecoming
in a department of the civil service. Official people must
speak in official language.

The Department's action in connection with the establishment of the Intermediate Certificate in the early years of this
century has, in certain circles, never ceased to be condemned.
By decreeing that all candidates for that Certificate, which
up to a year or two ago meant all pupils in State-aided
schools and in other schools preparing their pupils for the
full Leaving Certificate, must take Science and Drawing as
school subjects for three years, the Department, it is alleged,
effectively discouraged the study of Latin and Greek during
the years, between the ages of twelve and fifteen, when the
elements of these languages must be acquired if they are
ever to be studied with effect and real profit. With this latter
conclusion I agree so far as the pupil of average ability is
concerned. A genius can successfully begin the study of any
language at any age, but the normal student must do the
strictly " memory " work of Latin and Greek grammar when
his memorising faculty is at its best, between the ages of
eleven and fourteen. A further count in the charge against

the Department is that it accepted a pass in French as the equivalent in value to a pass in Latin for the purpose of gaining an Intermediate Certificate, although, the critics affirm, the former is much more easily secured than the latter.

Without elaborating the argument on the other side, it is only fair to state that something, in fact a good deal, can be said in defence of the Department's attitude and action. Reference has already been made to the neglect of the claims of Science and Art, as well as of French and most other modern subjects, not to mention English Literature, in the usual school curriculum of a quarter of a century ago, and the schools of the North-East were self-confessed and unabashed sinners in this respect. Perhaps nothing but compulsion could have removed such wilful, studied persistence in the neglect of modern subjects. Be that as it may, the Department compelled school authorities to " do their duty " in building and equipping Science laboratories and Art rooms, and at least for the last twelve years every school doing higher work has possessed the necessary facilities for the teaching of these very important subjects. It should be carefully remembered that up to 1921 every candidate for the Group Leaving Certificate had to take the Intermediate Certificate by the way, so that Science and Drawing were compulsory subjects for practically all pupils.

Presumably on the ground that these and similar subjects had been sufficiently established to maintain their places in school curricula, the Department waived the requirement of the holding of an Intermediate Certificate as a condition of study for a Group Leaving Certificate. Now the Intermediate Certificate has been definitely dropped. Pupils who are engaged in a full Secondary Course of five or six years are not now accepted as candidates for any school certificate except the Group Leaving Certificate. For such full-course pupils anything corresponding to the half-way Intermediate Certificate has absolutely ceased to exist. It may be stated parenthetically that pupils who have followed an *approved course* of post-qualifying education for three years and are leaving school may be presented for the Day School Certificate (Higher), a very unfortunate name for the school leaving certificate which testifies, without external written examination other than a two hours' general paper, to the satisfactory completion of such approved course.

The point at which we have now arrived is of first-rate importance for the purpose of our argument and our plea.

With the disappearance of the Intermediate Certificate a very large measure of freedom has been restored, and now is the time to forgive, to forget and to make a fresh start— a timely opportunity for those who have been partisans on either side as well as for those who were too little interested to range themselves with either host. Courses of a much less rigid kind may now be offered for approval, and it is hoped that full advantage will be taken of the freedom that is said to be in the act of being conceded. A word of caution may be permitted. It is much to be desired that no policy of retaliation be pursued by those who have been conscientiously opposed to the Department's " high-handed " action in the matter of compulsory Science and Drawing. The claims of Science, of Art and other " modern " subjects can in the twentieth century be neglected only at our peril. It is impossible to decide for a pupil at the age of eleven or twelve (which is the usual age of " Qualifying," that is, of passing from the Primary to the Higher Department) whether his bent is toward linguistic or scientific or other study. Every curriculum to be followed by pupils at that early age should preserve a just balance between subjects that are, after all, complementary, and should permit, and even encourage, specialisation to be postponed to a later stage when individual proclivities and predilections may have revealed themselves. The teaching profession is fully alive to the importance of the present issues. For some time those who are responsible for planning courses in Secondary Schools have been devising suitable alternative courses which they hope will meet the needs of various classes of pupils. Teachers have approached the problem without conscious bias in favour of literary or scientific courses. Now is the critical moment for all who have a claim to be heard to join in a constructive effort. May one who realises fully the importance of reasonable University autonomy, and who objects entirely to unreasonable bureaucratic interference, suggest that the University authorities, who already accept most forms of the Leaving Certificate as qualifying for University entrance, should co-operate more closely with the teaching profession in securing the recognition and successful carrying out of school curricula suited to the varying needs of all classes of pupils whatever may be their objective after their school days are over, and recognise for University entrance the application of any such duly-qualified candidate, without further test? The time cannot be far distant when a student's fitness to profit by University education will be judged solely by his record at school, and it is very desirable that Universities and the teaching profession should by common action hasten that day in a spirit of mutual understanding.

Frank and unfettered conference has accomplished much in many spheres of life in several national and international difficulties of recent years. A policy of standing aloof and of suspicion cannot justify itself. The interests concerned, those of the rising generation and of the extension and further diffusion of the higher learning in *all* its branches are too vital to be sacrificed to any feeling of *amour propre*. It may be stated without fear of contradiction that the prolonged fiasco in connection with the Entrance Board Regulations would never have emerged, least of all would it have been allowed to continue, if those who have taught and those who are going to teach the students had by means of representatives from both sides, actually in touch with the work, been brought into personal contact. The game of scoring petty points must cease. No really satisfactory solution of the seemingly difficult problem will be found until experts on both sides have applied their intelligence, their knowledge and their common-sense to its consideration. The abortive attempts made by the Board to carry out its statutory duty would be ridiculous if the interests at stake were not so important; but what language can be found to describe the unabashed autocracy of a body that is responsible for the policy that leads to the following naïve announcement on page 525 of the Aberdeen University Calendar for 1923-4? "By the Regulations of the General Council of Medical Education of the United Kingdom, *a body altogether distinct from the University*, every Medical Student at the commencement of his studies *should* be registered in the Medical Students' Register in the manner and under the condition prescribed by the Council." (In passing, I may be allowed to call attention to the word "should." Why is the direct "must" not employed?) Thereafter follow various rules and instructions for the carrying out of this fiat, also the conditions of examination and possible exemption, with a note of the fees for instruction and examination, the latter being apparently compulsory on all non-Graduates who have not passed a recognised examination. On another page of the Calendar is given the syllabus of work that must be overtaken by would-be medical students before they are registered. A minute examination of its terms has failed to reveal that the syllabus contains any branch of Science that is not professed in every Secondary School of reasonable size. Whatever adjustments might be found necessary would at any rate be both few and trifling, and yet the schools have had this programme and external-examination demand literally thrown at their heads without consultation by a body " altogether distinct from the University." In common parlance and in common decency "this is not good enough." No self-respecting profession could, in its own interests and in those of the pupils for whose education and welfare it is largely responsible, without a vigorous protest tolerate the wanton hurling of so serious an obstacle on the road that is supposed to be open between school and Scottish University. For any legitimate purpose, and especially to promote any end that will advance the interests of education, school authorities are willing to confer with a view to adopting their curricula to changing circumstances. In the case now under consideration every item of the syllabus can be taught in schools without any dislocation of the machinery, and the necessary examinations can be conducted by the present school and Inspectorial staff, whose members will doubtless welcome the active co-operation of University representatives who may be deputed, if necessary, to visit the laboratories where its pupils are at work. In this way much useful time will be saved; each student affected will have to spend three guineas less on his University education; and, most important of all from our point of view, a practical demonstration will be given of that co-operation that ought to characterise all the efforts of those who are responsible for the progress of learning at all its stages.

While the General Medical Council remained for years satisfied with a much lower entrance qualification for Medical Students than was permitted for students in the Faculties of

Arts and Science, the teaching profession continually urged an assimilation of the standards. Now the Council has gone to the opposite extreme and insists on the prospective Medical Students taking an extra course. Even worse, the student's knowledge must apparently be gained after school, at any rate he must pay a fee for attendance on a University class, and an additional external examination is arbitrarily thrust on these unfortunate entrants.

COMPULSORY LATIN.

THE question of the position of Latin in the curriculum of higher schools and advanced departments has been very much to the front in discussions on education in recent times. At least four abortive attempts of the Universities Entrance Board to carry out its statutory duty of fixing a test for intending University students have concentrated attention on the subject of compulsory Latin in the schools. The Board seemed to be of opinion that some knowledge of Latin must be demanded from every prospective Arts student. The judgment of the Privy Council in the matter indicated that such an interpretation of the Board's commission was much too restricted. What should be a matter of accommodation has unfortunately become a subject of acute controversy in which the protagonists are, generally speaking, the supporters of the traditional claims of the Classics on the one hand, and on the other the " Moderns " who support to a considerable extent the claims of the subjects once jealously excluded from the ambit of University study. The question is very far indeed from being a purely academic one. Neither schools nor Universities exist for their own sake. In a democratic age they must make it their aim to promote the highest educational interests of the commonwealth. If the Universities arrogate the right to pass regulations that entail injustice and hardship to the schools that prepare students for them, they cannot complain when a protest is uttered. It cannot be too often repeated that only a small proportion of the pupils who now complete the Secondary School course have the University as their objective. The school curriculum must, therefore, be planned on such lines as to provide suitable instruction for boys and girls on broad general principles without regard for the immediate vocation of sections of the pupils. Nearly all Secondary Schools have to prepare pupils for the University Bursary competitions. Their success as centres of education is judged to some extent by the appearance which their students make at these competitions. It is not unreasonable, therefore, that school authorities should ask that their views on a question that concerns them so nearly should be duly considered. I shall try later to show that the question of Compulsory Latin is of first-rate importance in its relation to the subject of competition for University Bursaries.

At the risk of being called a Laodicean, I have to state frankly that I refuse to classify myself among the classical supporters or with the moderns. I have read all or most of what Dr MacKail has said in favour of classical studies, and with one exception—when he says that classics are "necessary," I fail to understand what he means, or, understanding I refuse to agree—I homologate his conclusions, provided he will refrain from compelling us to teach Classics to *all* those who are following a full Secondary Course. I dissent entirely from the deliberately expressed opinion of the 1889 Commissioners that "the time occupied in acquiring a knowledge of Latin and Greek up to the standard of the higher grade of the leaving certificate examination was twice or thrice the time required to reach the same standard in French or German. In other words, the intellectual energy expended by the classical student was at least three times as great as that expended by the student of Modern Languages who attained the corresponding result "—(Strong). Having taught both groups for many years, I state baldly that the conclusion is ridiculous. A student who has passed on the higher grade standard in Latin and Greek can thereafter reach the same level in French and German in one-third of the time; but the Modern Language pupil can possibly do approximately the same with Latin and Greek. Immense harm has been done to the interests of Classical study by claiming that it must be compulsory. Once Classical study held the field. In our time it is only one of several options, most of which have substantial and proved claims to consideration as agents of culture and means of furthering national, social and individual progress and welfare. The protagonist who in these days declares that Classical culture is so immensely superior to any other that Latin *must* be the first foreign language taught in *every* school merely displays a profound ignorance of modern conditions in education and practical life, and does the greatest possible disservice to the cause which he champions. I may be forgiven for saying that I am so strong a believer in the virtue of a classical training that during the whole of my teaching life I have taught Latin to each of my six higher classes and have never allowed Greek to die out. But I do not believe in compulsory Latin, as some press its claim. I point out to my pupils at the beginning of their course that they have a chance of undertaking the study of a language which, in its initial stages at least, is not easy, but which is, in my experience, worth the expenditure of time and energy that its successful prosecution demands. That is all the "compulsion" that any teacher has a right to enforce; such is all the compulsion I find necessary. I ought to explain, however, that I do not now teach Latin and Greek on the lines that have made the North-East educationally famous. The intellect of a pupil of twelve years is too fine an instrument to be blunted by inconsiderate management. The Literature and the Language of Greece and Rome are something greater than lists of declensions and paradigms of verbs. To give all or most of the pupils under one's charge even a slight introduction to the delights and advantages that are possible to those who come into first-hand touch with the great Classical authors is, in my opinion, a much more sane and a much sounder method of procedure than to try to teach a few "bright" boys a "Melvin" version. While for their work's sake I admire all the dead and most of the living disciples of the Melvin gospel, I am convinced that their method was radically unsound, because it put the cart before the horse. Reading and comprehension must always come before reproduction. The Universities of Scotland cannot consistently demand that every intending Arts student must have passed an entrance examination in Latin. They sold the pass years ago when they offered, or consented, to award M.A. Degrees without Latin. Now they cannot wholly revoke the grant without doing serious harm to certain legitimate interests. In the interest of progress—I say nothing of consistency, which may be no virtue—they should drop all demand for "compulsory" Latin and adopt a policy that will better serve to promote real Classical learning. Let it be made known to all teachers, who are the really influential people in the matter, and to intending students, that the doors of the University are open to all who give satisfactory proof of possessing general culture such as may reasonably be expected from adolescents and such preliminary knowledge as is necessary for benefiting by attendance on classes approved by the Universities as leading to a Degree. Further, that while a knowledge of Latin and Greek on a recognised standard is of course essential for studying for a Degree that contains these subjects, such knowledge has been found to be exceedingly beneficial, directly and indirectly, to the average student who is to specialise in Philosophy, Modern Languages, English, History.

If I am told that this is not a heroic policy to advocate and pursue, I reply that there are more sensible and more effective things to do than " to die in the last ditch." The cause of the Classics is too strong to need supporting by insubstantial arguments. The policy I advocate is feasible and in line with modern conceptions. I trust the day is very near when the licence that has prevailed for several years in the choice of subjects for the M.A. Degree will be severely curbed, and students restricted to choosing from certain curricula planned from the point of view of culture and future service of the commonwealth. Having, however, gone so far, we can never go back to the rigid seven-subject curriculum of the pre 1890's. Though "compulsory" Latin —i.e., Latin for all graduates—is no longer a realisable ideal, very much can be done on non-compulsory lines to preserve the fine flower of Classical learning for a very large proportion of our students. The recent experience of France, which has had to recall the compulsory Latin decree, is very illuminating. A similar policy at home will lead to a like result. School and University must co-operate to secure a fair field and no favour for every branch of learning. The study of Latin and Greek by those who will really benefit by it has nothing to fear in such circumstances.

UNIVERSITY BURSARIES.

WE need to get back to first principles in the matter of the allocation of bursaries. Essentially a bursary is not a sum of money to be awarded on the result of a competitive examination taken part in by pupils whose circumstances may vary from comparative affluence to extreme poverty. Strictly speaking, a bursary should be the perquisite of the needy student. Bursary funds awarded to students who without these could secure a University education are in reality misapplied. We have come to rely on the method of competition largely because it is mechanical and therefore easy, but there are objections and abuses that leap to the eye. School machinery is thrown out of gear. The Bursary Competition at Aberdeen University requires that a successful competitor shall have studied five subjects all on the higher standard, and three of the five must be English, Latin and Mathematics. The Universities' Preliminary Examination is passed by means of four subjects, only three of which at most need be higher; the Leaving Certificate also requires only four subjects. The head teachers in the city and two adjacent counties were, till recently, and I believe still are, entirely opposed to the compulsory study of five subjects on the Higher Standard. They feel more and more that the Bursary Competition has become an artificial thing. They refuse, therefore, to have regard to the conditions prescribed by restricting their pupils to the subjects that will "pay," but plan varying curricula based on sound educational principles and keeping in view the capacity and future requirements of their pupils at the University and in the wider world. For they remember that we are living in a century which is democratic in outlook, in profession, and in actual practice for men and *women*, that there are diversities of gifts (which are not necessarily inferiorities) and of calling, and that therefore there must be

II

different methods of preparation for living in the widest sense, for work and for leisure. The pressure on the pupils is excessive. They have no time for relaxation, much less for developing their social and æsthetic instincts, for cultivating their individual tastes, for, in short, learning to live. In country districts where many boys and girls have to travel by cycle several miles daily or by trains which are often inconvenient, the expenditure of time, money and energy is far beyond what can be justified in the case of adolescents. A spirit of artificial rivalry is encouraged. The success of a school is judged by the number of its candidates that receive high places in the published lists, whether its attendance be four hundred or forty. Some pupils go forward in the fifth year, some in the sixth, some, gaining a comparatively high place, return to school for a sixth or seventh year to receive special coaching with a view to gaining the glory, which must be very small in the circumstances, of securing a place near the top. In no case is any account whatever taken of necessity on the part of the competitor, which cannot be regarded as desirable or as intended by the beneficent donor of the Bursary. For a well-to-do student to gain " glory " by securing a high place at a Bursary Competition may be defended; to " grab " funds intended for the necessitous student of proved ability but less opportunity admits of no valid excuse.

To these and other objections that may legitimately be put forward, it is no sufficient answer to say that the existing system has worked well on the whole, that the poor student has not suffered greatly, that rural students have gained at least their fair share of bursaries. Only those who are acquainted with the artificiality, the extravagance and the enormous cost to the individual student of the present method can fully appreciate the necessity of a change. A few suggestions are therefore put forward for the consideration and criticism of those whose minds are sufficiently open.

Let us plan to secure that, as far as possible, the requirements for entrance to the University, for Bursary Competition and for leaving School, shall be satisfied by one and the same test. That need not mean accepting the existing conditions for the award of the Leaving Certificate. No edicts of the Education Department are sacrosanct. The time is opportune for conference, adaptation and re-arrangement. But there must be frank recognition of the fact that there is in our time a great multiplicity of subjects, and that *each* of these has claims to attention in the schools and is making even greater demands on the Universities, which are with the utmost justice and reason continually asking for greater resources to carry on their present and prospective work. All interested—Universities, Colleges of every kind, Teachers of all grades, the Education Department, Education Authorities and the Carnegie Trust, whose Fee Fund has been so largely filched by the well-to-do to the serious loss of the needy—must co-operate without reservation or prejudice.

Is it a counsel of perfection to suggest that bursaries might be awarded largely on the pupil's school record, tested, on the lines already suggested, by those who actually teach, assisted by representatives of the Universities and others concerned? Several substantial advantages would accrue. Without encouraging or even permitting premature specialisation, the plan would allow a pupil who had received a good all-round education in the first four or five years of his secondary course to devote most of his time and energy during the latter part to the study of subjects which he found most congenial and in which he was likely to specialize. Regard could be had for the pupil's circumstances, his character and outlook. Bursaries could be awarded for one year only, and the money for this purpose might be supplied by local Education Authorities and bequests, which at present allocate considerable amounts for post-school education. In the second and subsequent years bursaries would be continued or discontinued, increased or decreased according to circumstances, performance, promise, &c. At the first and every subsequent allocation of a Bursary, regard should be had to the applicant's bearing at an interview with experienced, sympathetic investigators. In the business of life *savoir-faire* and *savoir-vivre* count for quite as much as intellectual acumen.

This system would make it possible to give greater assistance to students in the later years of their course. Many parents who have undertaken financial risks on behalf of their children find that their resources are unexpectedly diminished after two or three years' expenditure. In such

circumstances many a promising student takes a wrong—
the easy—turning at the end of the second session for want
of sound advice and promise of the necessary monetary help
to finance an Honours Course. A great desideratum of the
University at the present time is a thoroughly competent
adviser possessing financial powers, it may be in the way of
loans, and acquainted with prospects, for example in the
teaching profession with its urgent need of real specialists,
not pedants, in different departments of schools at home and
abroad. The world is calling for more "researchers," and
these can be secured if we will use wisely even our existing
resources. Another instance suggests itself in the medical
profession. May it not be largely for lack of wise advice
imparted at the right time that so few respond to the loud
call for highly educated men and women with noble aspirations to serve in the wide world abroad where the fields are
already ripe for the harvest but cannot be reaped for want
of workers? The suggested plan would also make practicable
a reform which, in my opinion, is urgent. The Universities
must make themselves responsible for the whole academic
education of future teachers. Training Colleges must become
training institutions only. That reform will save the
squandering of public funds on the education of some who
will never become efficient or effective teachers, and tend to
dissuade others from premature decision as to their future
profession.

This proposal will seem to some so novel and chimerical
that they will dismiss it without consideration. I grant that
it cuts right across most of the prevailing notions that govern
the award of Bursaries. I am so convinced of the soundness
of the idea that I venture to prophesy that within a reasonable
time a plan of this kind, or one conceived on similar lines,
will have been established by common consent. So far is it
from being revolutionary that in embryo at least it is already
to some extent acted on both in the University and outside
of it. I admit that it postulates an increased sense of responsibility and a determination on the part of all concerned—
University Authorities, elected representatives of the public,
and the teaching profession particularly—to utilise to the
best advantage the resources provided for the education of
the worthy and needy student whether by pious benefactors

or by all of us as taxpayers and ratepayers. The realisation of this ideal will be slow in proportion as we refuse to envisage the needs of the new age, but I am sure that it is worth consideration.

The four suggestions that follow apply mainly to Aberdeen University.

If it is too early to adopt that plan, this one is immediately practicable. Reduce the number of subjects for the Bursary Competition to four. Demand that each candidate take English, one Science subject, one foreign language and one other subject which may be either a foreign language or a Science subject; Science subjects being defined as Mathematics, Chemistry, Natural Philosophy, Biology. No one can assert that there is any injustice in such a scheme. It leaves sufficient room for choice on the part of every class of student whether his bent be Classical, Mathematical, Scientific or Modern Language. Admittedly it entails the necessity of strict supervision of the standard of examination and of correlation in marking and assessing the worked papers, but the solution of that problem should not be difficult.

Those who think that English as such should not be compulsory, but who desire to have some method of testing the applicant's intelligence and general knowledge, advocate that every candidate should have to take a General Knowledge paper which would include an essay. Thereafter each candidate would take four subjects, one of which at least would be scientific. In this case English would be one of the possible options like other languages. The plan is already in operation in Glasgow University.

In view of the need for securing students who will be capable of specialising later on, and who therefore might devote more of their time during their last year at school to the subject or allied subjects for which they possess special ability, somewhat of a reversion to a former plan is supported by some teachers. Let each candidate take English, then let him select three other subjects of which one shall be a Science, one a Foreign Language. Then he will take an additional paper in one of the four, with absolute equality of marks—*e.g.*, English Literature; Higher Mathematics—Analytical Geometry, &c.; more Advanced Latin, Greek,

French, &c. In the case of all languages, chief credit in the the additional paper should be given for first-hand acquaintance with the Literature.

The plan which I mention last has, in my opinion, very much to recommend it, if there must be a written competition. Divide Bursaries into classes with subjects somewhat as follows : —

(a) General: English; one other language; one Science; one other subject, which may be History.

(b) Classical: English; Latin; Greek; one Science.

(c) Mathematical: English; Mathematics; one other Science; one other language.

(d) Modern Language: English; other two Modern Languages; one Science.

I make no apology for including English in each group. No student should get an M.A. degree unless he has taken the English graduation class and made a good pass. Many graduates are notoriously ignorant of their own Literature, and the results are very manifest in too many who occupy positions of more or less importance in the "learned" professions.

If legislation is required to make some of these proposals possible, why should there not be legislation? There have been University Commissions before, and it is over thirty-five years since the last one reported, coming to some remarkable conclusions and making some very curious recommendations. In these thirty-five years the world has seen more changes— material, intellectual, social—than in any corresponding period of human history. No one can claim that we have reached finality or that our educational arrangements in School and University and in their mutual relations are perfectly or even reasonably satisfactory. Responsibility for the next step lies with teachers of all grades. The public is ready to trust real "experts" in education as in other matters. If by their own actions these experts show themselves worthy of receiving self-determination, the last vestige of external control will have disappeared in much less than thirty-five years.

THE EDUCATIONAL INSTITUTE.

ONE of the most striking features in the history of the last hundred years is the organisation of workers in various departments of activity. A century ago combinations of workmen were expressly forbidden by law. Even after the ban was removed the growth of unions was comparatively slow, but in the twentieth century it is the absence rather than the presence of organisation that calls for remark, and few of those who understand the conditions and problems of modern existence will deny that, on the whole, combinations and associations of those engaged in some specific industry or profession are calculated to promote, and do actually further, the legitimate interests of their members, and at the same time to contribute to harmonious relations with other organised bodies as well as to the promotion of the general welfare of the community. The doctrines of laissez-faire have had their day. All for each and each for all is a slogan more in harmony with modern ideas. One of the earliest formed of these associations is the Educational Institute of Scotland which has already played no inconsiderable part in Scottish educational history, and which, in my opinion, is likely to be more influential in the future.

The Educational Institute of Scotland was founded in 1847, and a Royal Charter was granted in 1851. The objects which the promoters had in view were threefold. They formed themselves into an educational association for " the purpose of promoting sound learning, of advancing the interests of Education in Scotland and also of supplying a defect in the Educational arrangements of that country by providing for the periodical session of a Board of Examiners competent to ascertain and certify the qualifications of persons engaged, or desiring to be engaged, in the education of youth in Scotland, and thereby furnishing to the Public, and to the

Patrons and Superintendents of schools, a guarantee of the
acquirements and fitness of teachers for the duties required
of them, and thus securing their efficiency and raising the
standard of Education in general." Of these three purposes,
the first two have always been, so to speak, the lodestars of
the Institute's activities. The third object has not yet been
realised. There is, indeed, no record of any attempt's being
made to supply the defect referred to. It may be questioned
whether the Institute will ever receive, or even claim, the sole
right of judging as to teachers' qualifications, but an increasing proportion of the more active members of the
profession hold that only when the Institute is officially
recognised as one of the two or three authorities jointly
responsible for the certification of teachers will the problem
be solved of securing an adequate supply of teachers for
every grade of pupil and all the different subjects taught in
school and University. I have dealt with this important
question in the chapter on " School and University," and I
have been assured that a considerable number of University
Professors are willing to co-operate with teachers in the
promotion of the movement for consolidating the ranks of
all engaged in teaching.

The Institute has done its best to hasten this desirable
consummation. Up to 1917 there were three associations
representing Scottish teachers, the Institute itself, the
Association of Teachers in Secondary Schools founded in
1885, the Scottish Class Teachers' Federation founded in 1894,
and each of these had its own organisation and officials as
well as its professional newspaper. In 1917, as the result of a
general conviction that the time was ripe for a considerable
advance in Scottish education and that Scottish teachers must
take a prominent part in discussing the underlying principles
and formulating the necessary plans, a Union of the three
associations was accomplished, and the Institute can now
claim that it represents at least four-fifths of all the teachers
in Scotland, including a number of University professors
and lecturers.

The supreme governing body of the Institute is the
Annual General Meeting which, in terms of the Charter,
must be held in Edinburgh on the Saturday after the third
Friday of September every year. Those entitled to be present

and to vote at the meeting number at present about four hundred, and, as delegates, represent the fifty-eight local Branches, whose membership varies from four in Tiree to over four thousand in Glasgow. Every item of business transacted during the year by any of the organs of the Institute is subject to review, within the limits of the Constitution and the Rules and Bye-Laws as laid down from year to year, by the Annual Meeting. The Institute is therefore a thoroughly democratic and representative association.

The strength of the Institute depends on the efficiency of the local Branches. Each of these has its own officials, comprising a President, a Secretary and a Treasurer, while larger Branches have several committees in charge of the more important departments of work. Meetings are held periodically for the transaction of business, for hearing addresses on educational and other topics of interest, for discussions on curricula, methods of teaching, promotion, standards of examination and other subjects dealing with school routine, and the social side is not neglected. The most efficient Branch is, of course, that which has on its roll of membership every teacher in the area, and the interest and enthusiasm of the officials of certain Branches are so marked that a non-member is a rara avis. In rural areas the difficulties of reaching the place of meeting are indeed formidable, but the prospect of meeting their fellows and of sharing experiences is sufficient inducement to bring out most of the really keen teachers.

Branches or combinations of Branches elect the large majority of members of Council, which is the central governing body of the Institute. The other members of Council consist of ten elected by the four Secondary Districts grouped round the Universities, of five returned by the Catholic Sections, and of the Office-bearers. The Council meets in Edinburgh five times a year for the purpose of transacting current business and particularly to review the work of its various Committees. The most important of these is the Executive, which is vested with fairly extensive powers between meetings of Council, besides, of course, being responsible for carrying into effect the decisions of the Council. Its meetings are held in alternate months in Edinburgh and Glasgow except in July and August, when only routine business is transacted by the officials. Of the Executive the most important sub-Committee is the Parliamentary, which, as its name indicates, is concerned with the relations of the Institute to the legislative and executive departments of government. Much of its work is carried out by deputations, and for its successful influence in the past it owes very much to the foresight and experience of its successive conveners and to the tact, political acumen and statesmanship of the Parliamentary Secretary.

There are nearly a score of other Committees, each of which is in charge of a definite department of the Institute's activities. The Benevolent Fund Committee meets as often as is necessary to allocate temporary relief to needy members, widows or dependants of members. From the yearly subscription of every member half-a-crown is devoted to the Benevolent Fund, and the Committee is thus able to be the constant channel of conveying the practical sympathy and material assistance of the profession as a whole to its members who have been stricken by sickness or misfortune. No fewer than eighty-five very deserving cases were helped by this fund during a recent year to the extent of about £30 each, the total disbursements for the year amounting to nearly £2,500.

The War Trust Committee administers the fund subscribed by Scottish teachers for the benefit of those of their number who suffered in the war or the dependants of those who fell. The most recent statistics show that the beneficiaries numbered fifty-three, among whom the sum of nearly £3,400 was divided. In all, therefore, these two funds help approximately 140 cases yearly at a cost of some £6,000.

One of the most necessary and active of the Institute's Committees is that which deals with Law and Tenure. Owing to their inexperience, heedlessness, sheer folly or other cause, at times it may be through the action of others, teachers sometimes find themselves involved in difficulties that may have unpleasant consequences for themselves and possibly for the profession. The Law and Tenure Committee is always ready to advise, caution, encourage, threaten, and even take drastic action when other means fail. It also conducts many very delicate negotiations with Education Authorities touching salary questions and all matters relating to tenure. Fortunately such difficulties are gradually becoming much less numerous since the disappearance of the smaller School Boards, which were notorious in too many cases for every habit and quality that should not characterise responsible bodies. The better relations now happily existing in the educational sphere must be ascribed to the Joint Council of Education Authorities and Teachers, which, though it has no executive powers, has proved itself a useful forum for the presentation of varying views as well as a means of taking united action for the furtherance of reforms that are found to be generally desirable.

The Secondary Education Committee can justly claim to be one of the most active and vigilant organs of the Institute. Owing to what teachers generally consider the foolish and short-sighted policy pursued by the Universities Entrance Board in recent years, there has devolved on this Committee the unpleasant task of leading the opposition to the Board's attempt to impose on entrants to the Universities restrictions that seemed to the Institute to be unfair and detrimental to the best interests of Scottish education, and the Institute had the satisfaction of finding that the Privy Council homologated the views put forward by the Secondary Committee and supported by other influential bodies. The Committee has recently concerned itself with such important topics as a new Geometry Sequence, Historical Research, the qualifications and salaries of those wishing to secure recognition as teachers in Post-Qualifying Departments, and in conjunction with the Primary Education Committee has been exceedingly active in examination and criticism of the proposals for the establishment of Advanced Divisions, the nature and content of the curricula for these, the responsibility for the award of the Certificate to be granted at the end of a recognised course and the qualifications, status and salaries of teachers engaged in Post-Qualifying Courses, both those making provision for language study and those of a more practical kind. The gulf between what may be called the official view and that of the Institute with reference to these Advanced Divisions is so wide that the Secondary and Primary Committees will, in all probability, have abundance of work to last for several years. Their efforts to find a satisfactory solution of the problem of discovering reasonably satisfactory alternative courses of as nearly as possible equal value for Post-Qualifying pupils of varying capacity and outlook should be sensibly aided by the investigations of the Research in Education Committee and by the experience of the Continuation Schools Committee. The latter of these has a long row to hoe before it attains its objective of securing that all pupils shall receive some form of continued education until they are at least sixteen years of age. The Research Committee has been for some years engaged in the investigation of such evergreen topics as qualifying promotion, periodical and terminal examinations and tests, speed in handwriting.

With the work of these four Committees is intimately related that of the League of Nations Committee. From the first the Institute has proved itself a zealous supporter of the League of Nations and its various developments, convinced as the members are that the principles of goodwill, conference and plain dealing on which the Covenant is based are exactly those on which the Institute has always laid stress. The Institute's active interest in the cause of International Peace is also shown by the prominent share it has taken in the carrying out of the arrangements for the meeting in Edinburgh in 1925 of the World Federation of Education Authorities. It is a striking tribute to the pre-eminence of Scottish education that the first gathering of this promising Federation should be held in our metropolis, which expects to welcome some hundreds of outstanding personalities from America as well as from most other lands.

The Finance and Publications Committee and the Organisation Committee have their attention directed principally to the business side of the Institute's activities. The Scottish Educational Journal is conducted on thoroughly up-to-date lines, and is increasingly establishing itself in favour with the members of the Institute. Proposals are being considered with a view to placing a copy of the weekly issue in the hands of every member. The Organisation Committee is expected to see that those teachers who have not yet joined the Institute, and those who for any reason have allowed their membership to lapse, are led to see that it is their duty to close the ranks. Only when all teachers are members will the Institute have an irrefragable claim to be representative of a united profession, claiming the right of self-government.

The Boards of Examiners and of Studies are recognised

by the appropriate authorities as the examining body for certain Preliminary Examinations, and the Board of Examiners is responsible for the admission of members to the Institute and for the recommendation to the Council and the Annual Meeting of persons considered worthy of the Degree of Fellow of the Educational Institute. As showing that the Institute is at all times ready to co-operate in every form of social activity, it may be mentioned that its representatives serve on the Scottish Council of Juvenile Organisations, the Central Council of the Workers' Educational Association, the Scottish Association for Mental Welfare, the Scottish Savings Committee and several other such bodies.

The officials of the Institute are six in number, the General Secretary and Treasurer, the Parliamentary Secretary, the Organising Secretary, the Editor, the Secretary to the Board of Examiners, and the Honorary Treasurer, all of whom are members of the Executive, as are the President, the ex-President, and the Vice-President. The President and the Vice-President are elected by the votes of the members of the Institute and hold office for one year. The position of the President is one of great honour and considerable responsibility. It is his duty to take the chair at all ordinary meetings, to represent the Institute at ceremonial functions in any way connected with education, to be a member of all deputations charged with the duty of looking after the interests of Scottish education, and to visit as many as possible of the Branches of the Institute.

The improved organisation of Scottish teachers in recent years has made possible a great extension of the influence of the profession on educational legislation and administration. Most of the reforms secured or foreshadowed by the Education Act of 1918 had been advocated by the Institute for several years, and the Institute's Reform Report of 1917 was more than an intelligent forecast of the succeeding year's legislation. Scottish teachers now occupy seats on most of the important administrative bodies, for example, Provincial Committees and the Central Executive Committee for the Training of Teachers. There are teachers' representatives on School Management Committees, and, of course, on Joint Councils in connection with individual Education Authorities, while two acting teachers are members of the Advisory Council of the Scottish Education Department.

In the developments that must take place in the course of the next few years, if Scotland is to retain her position, the organised body of Scottish teachers and individual teachers must take an increasing share. It is the deliberate policy of those responsible for Scottish education to give more weight in the decision of such important questions as promotion, standards of attainment, allocation of Bursaries, to the reasoned opinion of those who are in daily touch with the pupils. This policy has been abundantly justified by the striking progress that has been made during the present century in practically every branch of school education. Far more has been accomplished than would have been believed to be possible when one considers the low standard of attainment that used to be demanded from the entrants to the profession and the artificial methods that had to prevail when all progress was estimated by mechanical standards. The Institute has always been in the van of those who advocate advance. It has shown by its deeds that it believes the teacher to be the key-stone of the educational arch. Get thoroughly well-educated teachers, trained according to the most up-to-date methods, working under conditions calculated to make them proud of their position, reasonably free from material anxieties during their active life and after their retiral, and conscious of the trust that is committed to their charge. Only then will reasonable solutions be found for various problems that will always baffle the purely mechanical and the suspicious. The Institute still has as its principal aim the promotion and the extension of sound education.

THE TEACHER'S SUPPORT.

TO the solution of the various problems discussed in the foregoing pages the teacher is called on to contribute a quota which increases with the years. His importance in the school economy becomes ever greater. He may be less of an autocrat and choose, or be forced, to become more of a guide and a philosopher, but there is no doubt that the demands made on him by modern conditions of life are every year becoming more imperious. His charge is more varied in its composition than it formerly was, and it may be that from its variety it has become more interesting, but the load is one the successful carrying of which needs much thought and a deep sense of responsibility. The teacher of the future may, however, ease its weight in proportion as he avails himself of all the physical, intellectual, moral and social aids that are increasingly open to him. The difficulty or ease with which the Charge is carried will depend largely on the nature of the Support. As the load was considered from four points of view, let us deal with the carrying of it from these four aspects—Sense of Vocation, Personal Culture, Professional Solidarity, Width of Interest.

" If work is to be good there must be joy in it." It is said the craftsman of an earlier time took more pride in his work, and therefore got more joy out of it than the modern workman who tends more and more from economic and other causes to become a mere cog in a wheel. It is increasingly difficult to believe in and cultivate a sense of vocation, and yet for teachers, as for workers in every line of life, such a sense is a most valuable asset. The old masters inherited or cultivated this admirable pride in their work, and the extent to which they possessed it was largely the measure of their success. If teachers have lost or possess it to a smaller extent than they did, the cause of our ineffectiveness is not far to seek. Happy is the teacher who is a born teacher.

For him the day will be all too short. He will feel and know that this is his work, that no man or men can hinder, or even greatly help him in the doing of it.

Not all teachers, however, are conscious of such a call, and the presence of such a sense of vocation cannot reasonably be demanded from all applicants for admission to the teaching profession. Unhappy, however, will be the case of the person who voluntarily enters the ranks conscious of a distinct aversion to the work or whom contact with young minds neither enthuses nor inspires. Better far for him that a millstone were hanged about his neck, for he is taking upon himself an impossible task. Enthusiasm alone will not make a competent teacher, but it is certainly necessary if his pupils are to make real progress. He cannot communicate enthusiasm to them if he himself lacks it.

It is good that we should not overestimate our own capacity. Modesty in the young is both becoming and safe. Many successful teachers of the present day rather shrank at first from the responsibilities of the teacher's life, but they were encouraged by their own teachers who, during their school and college career, had noticed in them powers that, though latent, were capable of development. The unrevealed, perhaps unsuspected, capacity and energy needed stimulating and directing, and the commonwealth owes much to the prudent headmaster who selected his pupil-teachers not merely or even mainly perhaps for their intellectual powers, but for the less palpable qualities of sound character, sane outlook, and promise at least of sympathetic understanding of the child mind. Conditions have changed so greatly that neither the pupil-teacher method of selection nor the Junior Student system is any longer adequate to meet the needs of our time. But it is a mistake to think that the pupil-teacher system had no advantages. The pupil-teacher learned the art of teaching while young. He had to work or " clear out." He acquired life-long habits of diligence and self-reliance. Above all, he had to possess a sense of responsibility. The Junior Student, to whom we have bidden good-bye without regret, was rather encouraged to live a life of ease. To a considerable proportion of those who followed the course it seemed no discredit not to reach even the moderate standard of a Leaving Certificate, and an even larger percentage could pass through school and Training Centre without acquiring any reasonable sense of responsibility.

Those who desire educational efficiency are justified in demanding that there should be no special lure to induce students to enter the teaching profession. The full Secondary Course should be followed by all pupils without distinction or regard for their future profession. Only after that course has been successfully completed should pupils be encouraged, or allowed, to select their profession. The preliminary period of practical training taken at the end of the school course has been proved to be much more valuable in every way than the same amount of time spread over three years. Before finally deciding on a profession, all should be advised to continue their education at a University or a Central Institution, and thus let the impulse come unprompted as it comes to those who enter other professions. Needless to say, this principle should apply to all without distinction of sex. It is to be hoped that the differentiation introduced in 1924 in the conditions of training for men and women will speedily disappear.

It is a cruel kindness to recommend or encourage those who have no natural aptitude for the work of teaching, cruel to the applicants, to the pupils, to the profession. The unworthy and the unfit should be discouraged, dissuaded, debarred as early as possible. Teachers claim self-determination for the teaching profession, and on every ground of reason and justice they must press for it in the interests of educational progress. But the claim entails the deliberate shouldering of responsibilities which many in the profession are not yet prepared to carry. The profession must guard the entrance door. The profession alone has the knowledge and the experience required for the important task of rejecting the unfit and accepting likely aspirants. Promising recruits should be encouraged, and if the root of the matter is in them, their early diffidence, so far from being a disqualification, will gradually give place to some measure of confidence, and the sense of vocation will be developed by actual experience of teaching. Success, not superficial or meretricious success, will enhance this sense of vocation which is such a valuable, and indeed essential, support to the teacher in his daily work.

12

Sense of vocation may be inborn or, partly at least, acquired; personal culture can be neither automatic nor adventitious, if culture is understood and defined as "the love of truth, the love of beauty, the love of justice." It is difficult to decide how far capacity for the acquiring of culture can be or is transmitted, as experiment is impossible at a sufficiently early age. Nature and nurture are closely interwoven from the earliest months, and the strands are difficult to unravel. Probably, *very* probably, breeding tells here as elsewhere, and breeding is by no means synonymous with high birth. Undoubtedly environment counts for much in the development of character. Some educators declare that they will be satisfied if they are allowed full and unrestricted influence over the child only for the first seven years of life. The seeds they sow during that period in soil carefully prepared, skilfully manured and watchfully protected from noxious weeds and contagious pestilences will, they affirm, assuredly produce sixty fold. It may be that they exaggerate the permanence of their influence and the resisting power of the principles which they make it their aim to inculcate, but superficially at least history does not entirely refute the validity of the claim they advance. No one who has experience of actual work in school will try to minimise the importance of the effects of daily environment on the personal culture of the pupil. Whatever views we may hold as to the comparative merits of what are known as classical and modern systems of education, there can be no doubt that the up-to-date primary school is a much happier place for the pupil than the average school of thirty years ago. Generally speaking, it is true that the effectiveness of the instruction is in direct proportion to the pleasure that is found and the interest that is taken by the pupils in their work. The earlier we arouse in our pupils the desire for personal culture, the better it will be for them and us and the society of which they will soon become more or less important members.

As to the best means and methods of developing culture this is not the time to write, but a very slight digression may be pardoned. In recent times there has been much discussion of the relative advantages of Language and non-Language courses in Post-Qualifying organisation. Most teachers hold that for a certain type of pupil a course that does not include the study of a foreign language may be as educative as one that does. But there is a very great and imminent danger which reformers must try to avert if they can. "Advanced Divisions," if they are merely supplementary Courses slightly modified or even extended, cannot and must not be accepted as providing a satisfactory education for any class of Post-Qualifying pupils. Only if the accommodation and equipment are supplied on the same scale as is demanded for Secondary schools, only if the maximum number on the roll is the same, only if the teachers are equally well qualified, equally cultured and as well remunerated, can the proposals now made be accepted even temporarily.

Thus established and thus maintained, non-Language Courses may quite conceivably promote and develop the necessary personal culture even of the future leaders in different departments of activity, but those who realise the importance of good teaching should not be satisfied with any Secondary Course leading to a qualification as a teacher that does not make provision for the intensive study of foreign languages, and while they may and in fact need not advocate compulsion in the matter, they are justified in most urgently advising the intending teacher to take Latin right through his Secondary Course. The game is worth the candle many times over.

If in this connection I am reminded that in dealing with the Teacher's Charge I advocated that a certain type of post-Qualifying pupil might well receive what is for him the best kind of culture from a course that does not include the study of a foreign language, I reply summarily that there is really no inconsistency between my position then and my present declaration in favour of language study. There I was referring to a proportion of pupils whose school careers must of necessity be short; here I am concerned with future teachers, for whom we must provide the most liberal education that the Universities can supply.

The student who has been taught on sound lines, and who has applied himself with reasonable diligence at school and University, can hardly fail to have acquired at least the beginnings of culture, but the testing time comes later. Does he continue to be a student after he has become a teacher? In too many cases there is a dropping of study, a narrowing of interest. Personal culture can be developed by devotion to any subject, linguistic, literary, scientific, artistic, in particular by cultivating the fertile and inexhaustible field of English Literature as a means of personal improvement, of gratifying legitmate ambition and of acquiring influence. For this purpose, also, it is almost impossible to over-estimate the value of travel at home and abroad and of an interest in scientific, philosophical and other branches of research. And with all our striving after personal culture by study and other means let us not forget to have hobbies, two at least, so that we may not be bores to our friends. "Any rational interest which helps a man to shake off his fetters helps also to preserve his humanity and to keep him in touch with his fellows."

The effectiveness—not merely or chiefly the material success as measured by results and other mechanical but illusory standards—the real effectiveness of the teacher's work will depend on his personal culture to an extent far beyond the conception of those who have no experience of school work from the inside. Only those teachers whose minds are kept alert by such studies as will rekindle, revive and sustain their interest can hope adequately to influence those whose best possession is their sense of wonder still keen and undimmed.

A further support of the teacher is his membership of a great professional association. This section of the subject needs little more than mention here, as it has been already considered in the chapter dealing with the Educational Institute of Scotland. That members of a profession should keep aloof from the professional organisation should be unthinkable. The Institute is a democratic institution with a charter containing the five points, Annual Parliaments; Adult Suffrage, one member one vote; equal electoral districts as far as possible, and last (and greatest or least according to the point of view) Proportional Representation for the election of its Committees. When questions of the rights of certain classes of teachers present themselves for consideration, reasonable autonomy should be conceded, but we must preserve unity in substance as well as in name not by a condescending toleration, but by a frank recognition of our need of mutual help and of a common purpose as members of one body. For Professional Solidarity means much more than membership of the Institute, and we have not yet reached this desirable and necessary condition. We still talk of Primary and Secondary; Junior and Senior; Infant Mistress and University Professor, not always with frank recognition of the importance to the educational commonwealth of the other man's work. Ours is practically the only profession thus honeycombed. Diversity there may, indeed must, be; division and separation need not and should not exist. Each section needs the other for due deliberation, wise counsel and mutual help. There are problems that cannot be solved by any section alone, nor even by two or three, but only by all.

The individual teacher who is keen on his work and loyal to his professional colleagues has a claim on the support of his fellow-members on social grounds. In the course of my Presidential wanderings from Ayr to Shetland it was my good fortune to meet and be welcomed at Branch meetings by teachers who had travelled any distance up to thirty miles by road in order to be present. Hundreds of our members live in places far remote from what is called the centre of things. They desire to feel, and we ought to do what we can to help them to recognise, that they are not isolated units but members of a corporation to which it is worth while to belong. At Branch and other meetings all classes of teachers should contribute to formulating our policy so that the individual teacher may have the support of his fellow-members. What should be retained of the old, what should be adopted of new systems, should on broad, general lines be settled by the profession making use of the experience of its members of every grade. The Self-Determination to which we look forward, and which is so essential in view of the marked advance that is necessary, will be granted when we have prepared ourselves for it. Then we shall not need, we shall not be asked, to work a system which we have had no hand in devising or about which we have been graciously told *after* it was determined and when our criticism or approval was of equally little avail. Any Advisory Council consulted after a decision has been taken is a sham and a snare. We need a Council which has deliberative, deciding and executive functions. The real interests of education will continue to be sacrificed in proportion as we are weak in

Professional Solidarity and are in a position where we can with impunity be treated as the poor relation. Only a strong union enjoying the backing of all teachers is able to afford to its individual members that support which they both deserve and need.

Much has been spoken and written in recent times of the risk that teachers run through being in continual touch with children only, and thus of becoming narrow in their outlook. Even yet there is a sort of lurking suspicion that the school-master is rather different from the ordinary man. If there is any substantial ground for this suspicion, it is surely desirable that we should try to discover the cause and, if possible, find a remedy. For us, as for workers in every other department of activity, our own job must be our first and main concern. Failure to carry out adequately the work which we have been appointed and are paid to accomplish is a just and reasonable cause for our being condemned. On the other hand, our influence will be restricted, our efforts in school will not produce anything like their due effect if through conscious or unconscious neglect and failure to cultivate some outside interests, or owing to self-conceit, sheer laziness or indifference, we lose touch with the big world outside the school. We need continually and continuously to establish contact with those whose interests and outlook differ from our own. For this purpose holiday and refresher courses where teachers of different grades and from different countries meet; co-operative tours at home and abroad; educational conferences with some definite and limited objective may undoubtedly be of very considerable value. (There is, it seems to me, a very real danger that many modern conferences may be quite valueless, because there are too many of them, and because their platforms are too much frequented by long-winded cranks anxious for cheap advertisement.) Even more desirable and effective from the point of view of their influence on the teacher's outlook are periodical talks of a more or less informal kind, and meetings for formal discussion between teachers and members of other professions. Such symposia actually exist in some areas of Scotland, and the teacher members freely acknowledge the value of the "support" which they derive from their intercourse with the larger world.

Reference has already been made to the enforced isolation of many teachers and to the duty of the profession to do what it can to lessen this handicap. The parish schoolmaster of a by no means distant past had not much outside the school to inspire him. His services as general factotum in the district were much in demand and given without stint or hope of remuneration, but his spirit was too often crushed by poverty, lack of appreciation and studied neglect. A gradual change has come about in quite recent times, and teachers are now taking an interest and a full share in many kinds of activity outside the school. Such activities, carefully selected and restricted in number, have a most beneficial influence on the teachers and re-act very favourably on their work. In our corporate capacity and in our individual lives we shall do well to cultivate the wider outlook within the limits prescribed by the faithful performance of our daily work.

It is most undesirable that the Institute should ever ally itself with any political party. It will best consult its dignity and most effectively promote the chief end for which it exists —the welfare and advancement of Scottish education in all its branches—if it preserves an attitude of strict impartiality. There are, however, many organisations of a non-party, non-sectarian kind with which, it seems to me, the Institute's co-operation may and should be intimate and continuous. Among these I would mention such typical cases as the League of the Empire, the League of Nations, the World Federation of Education Associations as well as organisations of teachers in our own and other countries.

Practically every branch of knowledge has its recognised association, English, Historical, Geographical, Mathematical, Scientific, Art, Classical, Modern Language, &c. The support that may be derived from these is solid, and the advantages of membership to the individual teacher are numerous and real. Every community has its Councils, Institutes, Societies and other organisations which need and welcome the services of the best educated people in the district. Those among us who have devoted themselves to such work admit that from their connection with these bodies they have received more than they have given, and have been able, with some success, to help in creating a more favourable

attitude towards educational and other progress by co-
operating with the members of the community in advancing
general progress. Their "charge" as teachers has been
made lighter by the support they derive from the greater
width of interest.

Education has been aptly defined as the science which deals
with the world as it is capable of becoming. If we are
worthily to discharge the duty for which we have made
ourselves responsible, we must secure and use all the supports
available—knowledge and wisdom, imagination and sympathy, character and high ideals, a love of what is true, pure,
lovely and of good report.

Printed by Lindsay & Co., 17 Blackfriars Street, Edinburgh.